A

Christmas

Cracker

A collection of seasonal stories
from
Philip Whiteland

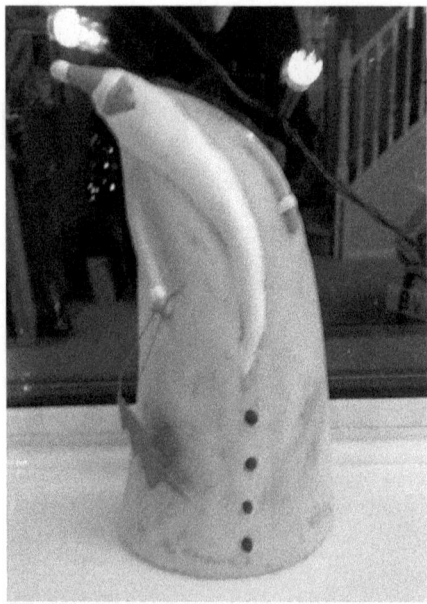

A leaning Santa...and why not?

A Christmas Cracker

Published by Philip Whiteland
Copyright ©2016 Philip and Hilary Whiteland
All Rights Reserved
This Print Edition published 2018

Also available as Kindle editions by this author:

Steady Past Your Granny's
Crutches for Ducks
A Kick at the Pantry Door
Giving a Bull Strawberries
The Things You See...

Cover design: John Steele and Philip Whiteland

In fond memory of Dennis

for whom Christmas and nuts were inseparable

Publication History

A number of the stories in this collection have appeared, in slightly different versions, in some of my previous collections, as follows:

Steady Past Your Granny's
My Christmas Presence
A Stable Upbringing

Crutches for Ducks
Coming to Town for Santa Claus
The Fag-End of the Year
It's a Gift!
You'd Better Not Pout...
Crackers at Christmas
Time, Ye Merry Gentlemen, Please!

A Kick at the Pantry Door
By the authority vested in me...
Lessons from Carols

CONTENTS

Introduction

A very dear friend of ours, sadly no longer with us (see Dedication) had a phrase he used to trot out on a regular basis. It was "Roll on Christmas...let's have some nuts!" He always said the last part with particular relish, as if he longed for the chance to break out the nut-crackers, despite the fact that he didn't have a tooth in his head and probably hadn't posed a particular threat to a nut for decades. It didn't actually matter what time of year it was, he could utilise the phrase on Boxing Day just as readily as he could in November.

Since his demise, I've rather adopted this phrase as a useful means of expressing exasperation, but it made me think the other day, do I actually want Christmas to roll on, with or without nuts?

I used to be a very big fan of Christmas. It seemed to me that it was the one time of year when, by and large, people behaved to each other as you would wish they would do at all times of the year. I think that's still true, although I suspect that the 'window of opportunity' is constantly shrinking. It was also the case that I was at my most enthusiastic about Christmas when I was footloose and fancy-free. It's relatively easy to be dewy-eyed about the festive season when your sole responsibility is to appear for Christmas Lunch relatively sober.

What I yearn for, and find harder to attain with each passing year, is that most elusive of emotional states, being 'In The Christmas Spirit'. This is impossible to define. It's a bit like love; you know it when you're in it. Of course, the advertisers of Christmas merchandise would really like you to feel ITCS from about August onwards, if the T.V. commercials are anything to go by. Their increasingly desperate attempts to engender this emotional state of mind actually have the opposite effect on me, and I'm sure many others. There is nothing more likely to promote an attack of the 'Bah, humbugs!' than a too-early Christmas-themed advert. I'm currently frothing at the mouth about a T.V. advert, in October, for Christmas hampers, not for this year's Christmas, but for the next one.

The purpose of this collection of stories is to help you, and possibly me, to achieve the state of being ITCS. I have always found Christmas, and the run-up to Christmas, to be a very productive time for writing, so I've gathered together a whole bunch of stories I've written about Christmases past and present, some factual, some fictional, over the years. Some of these, if you're a regular reader of my ramblings, you may recognise from previous collections, although I have made updates where it was sensible to do so. Interspersed with these familiar stories are others that have never previously seen the light of day, including a story featuring my two fictitious undertakers, written specifically for this collection.

This is a mix then of 'nostalgedy' pieces (nostalgia and comedy, if you haven't come across this term before) and seasonal fiction. I've really enjoyed gathering this collection together and I've been pleasantly surprised at the variety and range of tales that have built up over time. I really hope that you get as much enjoyment from reading these stories and that you're ITCS before you can say "Ho, ho, ho!"

Merry Christmas, whenever and wherever that may be, and I hope you get some nuts!

Coming To Town For Santa Claus

The similarities between Moscow and Derby may not be immediately apparent. Alternatively, they may be blindingly obvious, dependent upon your point of view and how well disposed you're feeling toward either destination at the time. All I can say is, that when I was in Moscow in the winter of 2005 (says he, place-dropping like mad), I was immediately reminded not just of Derby per se but of Derby at Christmas-time in the early 1960s.

The linking factor? Well, not the biting cold of winter or the grimness of the Stalinist architecture (no, I don't mean Derby!). The common denominator is, or rather was, the humble trolley-bus. They still have them in Moscow, along with trams, ordinary buses and, of course, a very ornate underground railway system.

The amazing thing is that all of these systems, along with the private motorist, still carry on working even when there is packed ice and snow everywhere and the temperature is - 260 C. In fact, the taxi I travelled in used his window-washer to clean his windshield – and it worked! Of course, it may have been filled with neat vodka for all I know but just see how well yours works if the temperature so much as plunges a couple of degrees below freezing (by which I mean your window-washer, in case you were making up your own jokes).

The sight of these wonderful old trolley-buses effortlessly carving their way through the, less than orderly, Moscow rush hour traffic was both inspiring and nostalgic. Inspiring, because it demonstrates just how effective our old public transport systems used to be, and could still be if they had not been cast aside. Nostalgic, because the last time I can remember being on a trolley-bus was on a visit to Derby with my Nana Whiteland, and we were on a mission to see Father Christmas.

I spent a good deal of time with my grandmothers when I was younger. My mum worked part-time as a typist and so, each weekday afternoon, during school holidays, I was allocated to one of my two grandmothers. Handily, my Nana Whiteland lived just a few hundred yards away from where my mum worked and close to my junior school, so I could call in after school to wait for my mum to pick me up.

I always enjoyed the build up to Christmas at Nana Whiteland's. She was an excellent cook and famed for her cake making skills. She would often be pressed into service to provide wedding and christening cakes. However, the sign that it was getting near to Christmas was when the large mixing bowl made an appearance on the living room table, along with a host of ingredients, and I was allowed to help with the laborious job of stirring the heavy mixture, laden with fruit, mixed peel and a liberal dash of sprits, into something that could eventually result in a Christmas Cake. The incentive to be involved in this was, of course, the chance to sample the mixture prior to baking.

The other culinary sign of Christmas coming was the mass production of mince pies. I've noticed, over the years, that mince pie production can become something of a competitive sport. At work, it was not unusual to find biscuit tins of mince pies springing up on desks throughout the office, their owners trying to tempt innocent passers-by with their wares, as if in some oriental bazaar. Success, amongst the mince pie fraternity, tends to be measured in terms of quantity, which is seen as a rough guide to quality. You've probably heard such things as "How many mince pies have you had to make this year, Doris?" (the implication always being that the cooking of mince pies is an intolerable burden, forced on the unwilling housewife by her demanding public), which then starts a bidding war which is always conducted in dozens (for reasons best known to this pastry-fingered posse).

Nana's mince pies were a seasonal legend, with pastry that melted in your mouth and a rich interior that was a meal in itself. When my Nana cooked mince pies it was almost on an industrial scale, such was the demand.

On this particular pre-Christmas afternoon, all cooking duties had been put to one side because Nana had an outing planned. We were going to Derby to do some shopping and, if I was very good, we might even see Santa Claus.

A trip to Derby, from Burton, was a real adventure in those days. People did not tend to move very far in any direction if it could be avoided and I had always felt that we ought to have our Passports stamped if we merely traversed the Ferry Bridge across the Trent to Stapenhill.

This trip involved a train journey into Derby, which made it even more of an adventure. At that time, travelling by train from Burton involved the grand old railway station much loved by Sir John Betjeman but, apparently, not so loved by the powers-that-be at British Rail as they pulled it down. Standing in the cavernous Booking Hall, waiting to buy our tickets from the dimly lit window, it was impossible not to be struck by the sense of grandeur of the building and the roar of the steam and diesel engines as they thundered underneath. This was clearly going to be A Journey. That this impressive building should have been replaced by something that looks like a redundant gent's toilet (by which I mean a disused toilet, not a toilet for redundant gentlemen) is one of a long litany of architectural disasters that have befallen Burton over the years.

Arriving at Derby, I can only remember dashing from one place to another on various forms of public transport as Nana set about her Christmas shopping with a determination that would have put Michael Palin's expeditions to shame.

One journey above all lives in my memory and that was, inevitably, the trolley-bus. To the best of my knowledge, we never had these in Burton and I was absolutely fascinated by this vehicle that looked like the unfortunate love-child of a tram and a double-decker, powered by a weird system of overhead wires and pantographs.

As our chosen trolley-bus whisked us noiselessly away, I wriggled on the moquette seating (not ideal for those of us still in short trousers) and watched the conductor as he jumped on and off the platform at each junction to wrestle the pantograph back onto the overhead lines with a long pole, all the while muttering dark oaths. Apparently my fascination with the trolley-bus was not shared by those who had to work on it, which may have been a factor in its demise.

I wish I could remember the Department Store that we went to for our visit to Santa Claus. My memory tells me that it was British Home Stores but others have suggested Debenhams. I'm sure readers with better memories may be able to correct me but the theme of this particular grotto experience was a Journey into Space.

I remember being terribly excited as we queued up to enter the 'rocket ship'. This was a separate room from the rest of the shop, accessed through a doorway covered by a dark curtain. Inside the room were two rows of double seats on either side of the 'rocket' and a series of portholes in the walls.

Nana and I settled down on some seats on the right hand side of the craft and soon we were preparing for take-off. The countdown began, there was the noise of rockets firing, and then the stars and planets began to flash past the portholes as we hurtled into space. I have to say that it was all very realistic for a youngster in the early 1960s. There was a real sense of motion and excitement. Nowadays, they would probably laugh themselves senseless at the sheer low-techness of it all.

When we 'touched down' on our destination planet, which I suspect was the Moon (and quite why Father Christmas was on the Moon in the first place was never really explained), we trooped out through the curtain at the prow of the rocket and into a grotto containing the man himself and a few assorted elves.

Now it would make a much better story if I could say that he reeked of booze and fags, or fell off his sleigh, or anything really but I'm afraid that would not be true. I simply collected my present (probably a colouring book and crayons – that seemed to be the gift of choice in those days), said "thank you" as required and then was escorted out by a passing elf. The whole effect of being on lunar soil was somewhat spoiled by the fact that, once we were on the other side of the curtain from the grotto, we found ourselves on a flight of stairs that took us back to the, less than interstellar, sales floor.

We made our way back onto the dark, damp streets of Derby with the lights of the cars, buses and trolley-buses circling around the town (in its pre-city days). Standing on the pavement, clutching my present, I could just about believe (with that firmness of belief that only children can truly muster) that I had been to the Moon and had seen Santa Claus.

Somehow though, I knew that my abiding memory would not be my interstellar adventure, it would be a disgruntled conductor wrestling with a long pole to reconnect one of the quirkiest forms of transport I had ever seen. I wonder if the young Muscovites of today feel the same way?

The Fag-End of the Year

Christmas is the time of year when television adverts really start to annoy me. For most of the year they are often brief oases of originality in the great desert that is popular television but, come January, you are either taunted by sale offers, in which the things you queued for ages to get pre-Christmas (and paid a very high price for) can now be had for half the price and with free delivery. Or you find yourself nagged relentlessly to undo the over-indulgence they were encouraging you into just a few days before.

I wonder if there is a benighted furniture store somewhere that is forever doomed to offer sofas and so on at pre-sale prices, just so that the others can quote them? If there is, I'll bet poorly performing managers are threatened with it, "You'll have to buck your ideas up, Wayne, or it's Scunthorpe SofaCentre for you my lad!"

Between the cut-price sofas and bargain-basement electronics, the average viewer can now be encouraged to lose weight painlessly (and apparently without giving anything up) or can be chivvied into stopping smoking using a bewildering panoply of aids, from chewing-gum to patches and helplines to hypnosis. Now, as an ex-smoker myself, I am all in favour of rescuing more people from the wet and bedraggled gangs that can be found outside every pub, club and office block, but it does amaze me how far things have changed since my smoking days.

It is hard to recall now just how ubiquitous smoking was in the 1950s and 1960s, when I was growing up, right into the 1970s, when I was a firm link in the nicotine chain gang myself. It is difficult to say anything positive about smoking, particularly these days when you're liable to be hung, drawn and quartered if you even suggest that there might have been something pleasurable about it. One thing that can be said is that it certainly made Christmas simpler. Why? Well, if your intended present recipient was a smoker, then a whole world of potential gifts opened up before you.

Do you remember, for example, those massive gift packs of cigarettes that were standard Christmas fare not so many years ago? From Boxing Day onwards, most smokers were wandering around with cigarette packets the size of laptop PCs, containing 100 or more cigarettes in neat rows. These packs were hopelessly impractical for everyday use but were an absolute godsend if, like me, you were an impoverished student who spent most weeks trying to spin out a pack of 10 Players No. 10 from one pocket-money day to another.

If smoking products and accessories were going to be your gift of choice, then your first stop had to be your local tobacconist and, if you lived in Burton, then the tobacconist of choice was Frederick Wright's on High Street. This was a sort of nicotine nirvana for anyone interested in tobacco-related purchases.

The beauty of buying gifts for the smoker, in those days, was that there was such a vast array of paraphernalia that could be attached to the habit. There were table lighters, pocket lighters, novelty lighters (often in the shape of a gun, which is a tad ironic), cases for cigarettes, cases for cigars, ashtrays ranging from the spectacularly decorative to the everyday functional, stopping off at novelty along the way. I always used to be fascinated by those where you stubbed a cigarette out on a metal plate and then pressed down on a plunger, whereby the detritus was whisked away by centrifugal force to the bowels of the ashtray beneath. You could also have matchbox holders, cigarette holders, pipes, pipe cleaners, tobacco bowls and so on and so forth, and that's without even considering snuff.

The first thing that assailed the potential customer on entering Frederick Wright's (and it was always known by its full title for some reason) was the rich smell of pipe tobaccos and snuffs exhibited in wooden bowls all around the shop. If you had a particular desire for a personalised tobacco mixture for your pipe, then Frederick Wright's would be happy to weigh up a mixture according to your precise instructions, and I believe many did.

If you wanted to appear really cool, then you could purchase Cocktail Cigarettes in a variety of fluorescent colours, pinks, greens, blues etc. with gold filter tips. I imagine these were intended for discerning female smokers to puff on between Ferrero Rocher at the Ambassador's party. Men could indulge their James Bond type fantasies with black Balkan Sobranie cigarettes and a lot of my friends invested in these in an attempt to buy an aura of sophistication for Christmas parties.

Being permanently broke, I never reached these dizzy heights but I did go through a rather pathetic phase of trying to imitate the effect by encasing my Players No. 10 in liquorice paper. Do you remember liquorice paper? It was a variety of cigarette paper intended for 'rolling your own', something I was frequently reduced to when an excess of week over money occurred (and we'll have no lewd sniggers at the back there, thank you).

The overall effect of wrapping one cigarette in yet another paper tube was to have your own portable bonfire, with a similar effect on the taste. However, this was about appearance rather than aesthetics and, anyway, in those days I would have smoked dried tea-leaves if I thought it would work. Some of my friends did and most of them are still here to tell the tale.

Then there were the vast range of cigarettes. From industrial-strength working-men's fags like Players Weights, Senior Service, Capstan Full Strength, Navy Cut, Park Drive (a personal favourite, I always described it as the working-man's cigar) and Woodbines, to the more 'exotic' and continental such as Peter Stuyvesant and Camel in the flexible packs and Passing Clouds 'Turkish' for those who liked their smokes to look as if someone had already sat on them.

Of course plain cigarettes, i.e. those without any form of filtration system, were a real exercise in dangerous smoking. By this I don't mean just the accumulated gunge that was allowed to sail straight into the lungs of the plain cigarette smoker, although that's bad enough. I mean the attendant problems that plain cigarette smoking brought with it, such as the cigarette becoming unexpectedly welded to your top lip.

The outcome of this unfortunate occurrence was one of two scenarios. Either you confidently pulled the cigarette from your lips only to find that a good chunk of your lip was still attached to the cigarette in question (not for the squeamish) or, and potentially worse still, you pulled the cigarette but it remained glued to your lip causing your fingers to slide down the cigarette and remove the lit end, with some force, to pastures new. If you were simply walking down the street then this was simply embarrassing and painful. If you were driving a car, however, then it was potentially fatal. Believe me, answering a mobile phone whilst driving may be overly distracting but is as nothing compared to the sure and certain knowledge that, at any moment, your lap is going to burst into flames as you're hurtling down the outside lane of the M1. Plain cigarette smoking would nowadays be classed as a dangerous sport that would give bungee jumping a run for its money.

Now that we live in more health-conscious times, tobacconists like Frederick Wright's must be very few and far between. I dare say that our grandchildren would be horrified at the thought of every social event being shrouded in a thick pall of cigarette smoke and of tobacco-related products forming a standard part of the pile of Christmas presents. Alternatively, as they open their fifteenth gift-wrapped shower gel or pack of socks, they might secretly wish for the shock and horror that opening a pack of 100 Park Drive might cause on Christmas morning.

To those of you struggling with your nicotine abstention and bitterly regretting your decision to "give it up this year once and for all", all I can say is that it does get better, your health will improve, and do you really want to burst into flames on the motorway?

It's a gift!

Each Christmas Eve, just as the shops are getting ready to close, you'll see a fraught group of individuals (usually men), beads of panic-induced cold sweat forming on their furrowed brows as they fruitlessly search for 'the perfect present'. I speak with some authority here, as I used to be at the head of this procrastinating pack and I know the iron grip on the intestines that develops as you realise that this year's 'must have' children's present cannot be obtained for love, money or impassioned pleas, as it sold out in October!

It seems to me that it is getting more and more difficult to buy something novel and engaging for the average child these days (if there is such a thing as the average child). For example, I have two nephews (neither of whom at the time of writing had attained school age), who could easily open their own toy shop with the collection of gifts they have accumulated over their few years. Yet, with each passing celebratory event (Birthdays, Christmas, Easter etc.) more devices and gadgets are prised into the groaning toy box.

Now, before you turn the page, tutting about another old fogey enviously trying to ruin a child's fun, I would like to reassure you that I'm not of that mindset that believes that a bag of marbles and a whip and top is all that is required for endless hours of amusement. I could never figure out what you had to do with a whip and top, and I lost my marbles years ago. I know that, as a child, I would have crawled over hot coals and broken glass to get at some of the toys available today, in fact, I probably still would. I just think that the sheer quantity means that very few of these high-tech gizmos are ever really valued.

High-tech is, of course, the operative phrase for most toys today. Everything designed for 0 years upwards seems determined to educate the unsuspecting child to within an inch of its life. Each toy that you pick up feels the need to talk to you, play a song, flash a series of coloured lights or do all of the above.

My abiding memory, from that time of life (0 years and above), is of a string of plastic lambs stretched across my pram (depressing, isn't it – I would be hard pushed to tell you what I did yesterday but I can remember a string of plastic lambs from my pram).

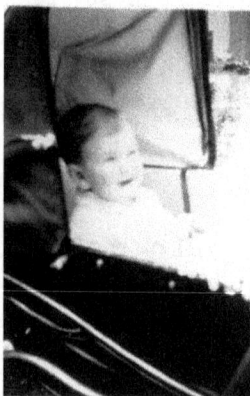

Philip at 10 months old – don't think the plastic lambs are in there

These were of different bright colours and they rattled when hit. That was it. They did not illuminate, play tunes or try to school me into remembering basic words and numbers. They rattled. They were great to chew with inflamed gums. I loved them.

I certainly had more than my fair share of toys over the years, although some had been 'previously loved', to quote a current euphemism. Not that this made any difference to me, after all, a toy is a toy is a toy.

I remember one particularly stunning Christmas Day, when I unwrapped the presents from my parents and found not only a train set but also a Scalextric set. That these were second-hand did not occur to me until much later when I realised that my Scalextric cars had a certain post-war style. Each had a large metal wheel at the centre that slotted into a similarly large metal groove in the very robust plastic track. My contemporaries had tiny stylish plastic Formula 1 type cars that zipped around a lightweight track, whereas strong men could have developed hernias setting out my system. The transformers hummed alarmingly and the contacts between the power source and the track, formed by bending bare wires around small metal spikes, meant that races frequently ground to a halt when the contact wires came adrift. But it was a lot of fun and I wish I still had that set today; it would probably be worth a small fortune!

Probably the most traumatic present I ever received was also the most expensive. Mrs. S., the wife of my mum's boss, took it upon herself to take me into town to do some shopping (I would be about 7 at the time). At the end of this shopping trip, we went into Woolworth's in its former location on the High Street (roughly where the Lord Burton pub is today, if you know Burton upon Trent).

Do you remember the smell of beefburgers that used to permeate Woolworth's in those days? Woolworth's had their own snack bar by the rear entrance (which led onto the Memorial Gardens) and a speciality was their own beefburger, which resembled nothing that I have tasted before or since but which was very popular in those pre "do you want fries with that" days.

Anyway, I digress. Mrs. S. took me to the toy counter of Woolworth's and told me that I could have anything I wanted from the counter! I was stunned. Faced with this cornucopia, I was spoilt for choice, but my eye had been taken by a toy small metal aeroplane whizzing around above an airfield, on a thin wire. The toy was bought and I hugged it all the way home. Mum, however, was beside herself with embarrassment. The toy I had chosen happened to be one of the most expensive available and mum (despite Mrs. S's assurances that this wasn't a problem) felt that I should have been more frugal in my desires. The toy remained a symbol of my childhood greed for some time. In actual fact, although I played with it a great deal, it was a little limited in entertainment value.

It consisted of a contoured metal landscape base depicting an airfield and surrounding countryside. At the centre was a conning tower (that shows my age) from which came a thin wire, at the end of which was a small aeroplane. The whole thing was powered by clockwork. By means of a control panel at the front of the base, it was possible to adjust the altitude of the aeroplane and its attitude to the ground. Nevertheless, even with the most active of imaginations, it was difficult to hide the fact that the only thing the aeroplane did was go round and round remorselessly until the clockwork ran out.

Another toy that was considerably cheaper but had much greater scope for imaginative play was called "Driving Test". I don't know if you remember this? Basically, it was a cardboard box on which a series of roads, roundabouts and cul-de-sacs had been printed. A plastic control lever at the front controlled a pantograph with a magnet beneath the surface of the box. Using this control lever, it was possible to manoeuvre a small plastic car (with a metal disc on the underside) around the road layout. The joy of this was that there was no traffic, pedestrians or any other three-dimensional obstacles to take into consideration. Therefore, it was entirely possible to reverse into, say, a shopping precinct without any consequences (you would be amazed at the fuss some people make if you do this in real life). I loved this toy and could play with it for hours. I'm not sure that it did much for my driving ability as it took 3 years and 3 tests before I was let loose on the unsuspecting road-going public, but give me a joystick and a plastic car and nothing could stop me!

The type of present most children secretly dread is the 'useful' present. It's difficult to look enthusiastic about a pair of socks or a pencil case. However, one 'useful' present I received did stand the test of time

It was Christmas, 1962, and Mum and I had slithered and stumbled our way through the thick snow and ice from our home in Anglesey Road to my Auntie Vera's house in Branston Road. When we arrived, Auntie Vera told me that Father Christmas had been to her house and that she thought he had left a present by the fireplace in the spare bedroom (look, I was 8 and I still believed – and why not!) I dashed upstairs and there, by the fireplace, was a large brown paper package. Unsure of what to expect, I eagerly unwrapped this giant parcel. At the heart of the brown paper and string, I found a dressing gown. Now, it's hard to be excited about a dressing gown when you're 8 years old. It's not that easy when you're 48. But this was no ordinary dressing gown.

Auntie Vera was a fantastic self-taught tailor who could turn her hand to virtually any type of needlecraft. She had found a small quantity of camel material (no, it didn't have two humps in the back) and had decided to see if she could make a dressing gown. The end creation had broad lapels, deep pockets, saddle stitching all around the hems and, best of all, a chest pocket onto which my initials had been monogrammed. It was warm, stylish and I felt great in it. At that time, it was a full-length garment. By the time I finally parted with it, 6 years later, it was more of a smoking jacket after the style of Noel Coward, but to me it was as good as it was on that first Boxing Day. If anyone wants to know why the cult of personality looms large with me, I blame the monogrammed dressing gown!

So, next Christmas Eve, when you're agonising over some flashing, whirring gizmo that is trying to 'stimulate your playing experience' in an annoying American accent, just remember that the most memorable present you could buy might not consist of anything more than a clockwork aeroplane, a magnetic car or even a monogrammed dressing gown (batteries not included). Just don't blame me when your children/grandchildren are looking at you accusingly on Christmas Morning.

Philip with a Christmas Gift from another age

Gift Wrapping

I'm a big fan of presents. This may seem like a statement of the blindingly obvious, but bear with me.

I'm a big fan of presents before they've been opened. All of those boxes and odd-shaped parcels in wrapping paper, bows and gift tags are such a wonderful sight because they have the potential to be almost anything. Stripped of their wrapping and decorations, what you essentially have is a pile of someone else's shopping.

Very odd shopping it can be at times, too. Just remember, when you're looking in wonderment at a bottle of something quite strange and usually involving fruits, spices and other bizarre ingredients, that this is something your friend or relative thought you might like. What does that say about you...or them? Now all you have to decide is whether to drink it, shower in it or add it to the 'Present Drawer' to be given to some other unfortunate next year. Don't try and tell me you don't have a 'Present Drawer', it's everyone's guilty secret! Thinking of this caused me to reflect on some presents I have received over the years.

I remember being particularly pleased to receive a portable radio when I was 8 or 9. Whether it was portable or not was open to some debate. In this case, portable meant 'as opposed to normal wireless receivers' which, in the early 1960s, were still the size and design of small sideboards. It could, apparently, work off the mains or a battery. However, the battery turned out to be something that could start a small car, and also cost a fortune, so the mains option was really it.

Another present I enjoyed was a Waddington's game called Careers. Why I finished up with this, rather than Monopoly, is a mystery only known to my parents. Perhaps Toyland, in the Market Place, had sold out of the popular games? Certainly, I never met anyone, before or since, who had this game or had even heard of it. Instead of growing rich by speculating on property in London, you tried out various occupations, usually of an unlikely but attractive nature like astronaut or beauty queen. Presumably options for accountancy, quantity surveying or sewerage management (another form of quantity surveying) had not proven popular in trials. At the end of each 'career' you collected a salary and there were opportunities for bonuses and prizes. It tells you something about me, that the paper money for this game was still pristine years after I first had it.

Compendiums of games were a 'value for money' option which used to be a staple children's present. It was one of these that provided a modest income-generator for me, in the form of a mini roulette wheel and gaming board, with which I took great delight in learning all of the various odds for the potential bet combinations. When we kept our pub, it was not unknown for a select band of dedicated drinkers to stay on past closing time and join us in the living room for a 'nightcap' or two. If I happened to have the roulette wheel set up (and it was odds on that I had), then I could usually be 'persuaded' to let them have a go for the odd penny or halfpenny bet. It's almost impossible for the Banker to lose at roulette, so this usually resulted in a profit which could go toward the purchase of more D.C. or Marvel comics to add to my collection.

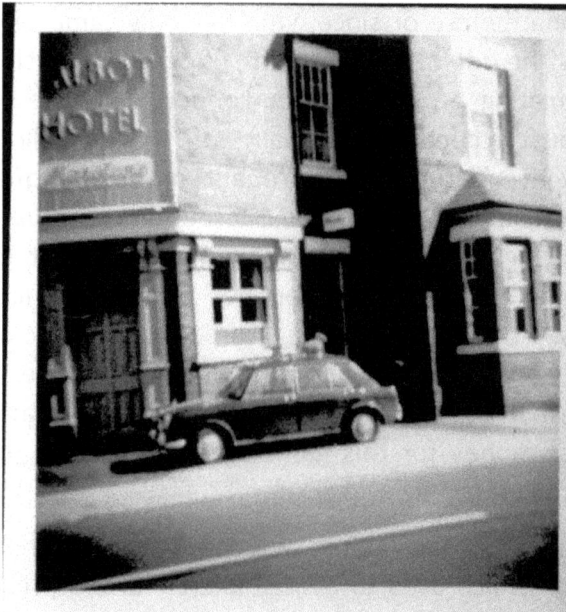

Our pub, The New Talbot Hotel, as it was in the 1960s

The other game that attracted the attention of the gambling fraternity in our pub, was Escalado. Remember that? It was a horse racing game that today's children, with their tablets and gaming consoles, would find laughable. It consisted of a length of green cloth, with little rows of stumps at regular intervals, which substituted for fences. At one end of the 'racecourse' was a box containing a ratchet with a handle on top. Metal horses of different colours were then placed on the cloth, and the action of turning the ratchet caused this to vibrate and the 'horses' to advance toward the finish line, or, more often, fall over. It was an extremely noisy game but it could engender quite a bit of competitive rivalry amongst the punters and, in the same way that you've never seen a poverty-stricken bookie; it ensured a steady flow of funds to me.

Something else that you often used to see in a child's Christmas Stocking were those 'Smoker's Companion' chocolate sets. These were like a Selection Box but used very cheap chocolate made in the form of meerschaum pipes, books of matches, lighters and, of course, paper-covered chocolate cigarettes. I used to really like these, particularly the chocolate cigarettes which looked the part. I should think you would be frog-marched to the nearest cell if you tried to market such a thing now.

Junior Conjuring sets were also popular, although these often required a considerable suspension of disbelief by the adults subjected to your display of digital dexterity.

Another toy requiring the suspension of disbelief was a ventriloquist's doll I received one Christmas. In all honesty, I think this had more to do with my dad wanting one, but beggars can't be choosers. I obtained a book on ventriloquism for children and, with a great deal of highly annoying practice, became passably acceptable at it. Although my lips may not have moved (much), I adopted a fixed, unconvincing grin that made me look like someone who had been embalmed before his time. Nevertheless, I was good enough to amuse my sister when she was small, so I was interested to see if I could still manage the same for my new grandson whilst he was still at that happily uncritical stage.

Apparently not!

By the authority vested in me...

If you are currently wondering what to get for the man in your life, for Christmas, birthday or any other significant occasion, then I'll let you in to a little secret.

For a start off, you can forget all of your power tools. You can certainly forget them as far as I'm concerned. I have spent a good deal of my existence getting rid of tools, power-driven or otherwise, in the certain knowledge that I'm a lot safer without access to these. You see, if I have tools in my possession, then it's only a matter of time before I persuade myself, or someone persuades me (more likely) that "it's only a simple job, I'm sure you could manage it". If you don't have the necessary tools in the first place, then you can't do it and, hopefully, the evil moment will pass. Otherwise, you can finish up in the same position as someone I know who, during various spells of unemployment, has systematically demolished his own house from the inside.

Anyway, back to my original point. Forget power tools, forget also 'smellies'. We don't mind these but the problem is that we never wind up with a set of complementary products. We may start with such a set, of course, perhaps bought by some generous aunt or sister, but, in due course, various elements will run out whilst other, less useful, elements linger like a constant rebuke. Face Scrub, for instance, may prove to be surprisingly long-lasting, whereas anti-perspirant or shower gel will vanish like butter in the sun. The end result is that these are then replaced by various ad-hoc presents during the year which will, inevitably, be of an entirely different fragrance. This means that the average man, if he wears anything at all, is likely to be the olfactory equivalent of a contemporary jazz ensemble, with each player adding an entirely different tune.

So, we've established what not to get? Well, almost. Clothes are also a no-no, because we will be inclined to wear them. Even after the first trial session, when you realise with a sinking heart that you have bought something for the shape that you would like him to have, not the shape he actually has.

No amount of "I could change it if you don't like it" will make any difference. In fact, the likelihood of the man in your life holding on to it grimly and insisting that he absolutely loves it will be in direct inverse proportion to how unsuitable you now think it is. Thus, that skin-tight pullover that you now realise makes him look ten months pregnant, will be the best thing you've ever bought him because, when he looks in the mirror, he sees the shape that he thinks he has and that you remembered when you bought it. The impact of fish and chips, pints of beer and zero exercise is entirely and wondrously discounted by the magical stretching abilities of modern fabrics.

Just whilst we're on this topic, why do some women of a certain weight insist on wearing clothes that are bound to emphasise the avoirdupois? Amazingly, skin-tight leggings do not have a slimming effect and neither do horizontal stripes, crop-tops or min-skirts. I'm not saying 'wear a sack and have done with it'. It's perfectly possible to be a little short for your weight and still look elegant and attractive. I accept that, according to my weight, I should be 7' 2". Mind you, I'm neither elegant nor attractive.

Now, where was I? I do seem to have wandered quite a way off my original point. Oh yes, what to buy the man in your life? Well, it could be Viagra, then you could get some life in your man (boom, boom, as Basil Brush would say) or, if I could make a humble suggestion, how about a high-visibility vest, a two-way radio and, if you really want to go the whole hog, a pair of reflective sunglasses. Let's take the rationale for each of these suggestions in turn.

Firstly, the high-vis (to quote the vernacular) vest. These items of clothing instantly convey power to the wearer, possibly even super-powers! A man with a high-vis vest can stop traffic, literally. Put him at the entrance to anything and he has the power to interrogate. "What are you here for today then, sir?" No-one ever questions his authority to do this, the high-vis vest is sufficient unto itself. Every man, secretly, wants a high-vis vest, and the best of it is they are incredibly flattering. No matter how portly or scruffy the wearer, the donning of the magic vest renders all beneath it authoritative, commanding and superior.

Then there's the two-way radio. Am I alone in thinking that the vast majority of the conversations conducted via these are entirely superfluous? Such stuff as:

A: "Jim, come in, over"

B: *Appallingly loud static noise, brief snatches of music, then faint but unintelligible sound that just might be speech of some form or another*

A: (*looking knowledgeable*) "Roger that, Jim. Just checking that the radio is working, over"

B: *Even worse static noise followed by a noise like a whale in distress, then something like a vacuum cleaner on reverse suction.*

A: (*chuckles knowingly*) "Yeah, 10-4 Jim. I can eyeball that for sure, for sure, over and out"

Even though it generates such inane rubbish as this, most blokes would give their eye-teeth (what are these, and why are they so valuable?) to have one. Well, two actually, one being of no use at all. I can speak with some authority on this as, at the time of writing, I'm on a cruise (bear with me, I'll explain). Quite a number of parents on board have taken the sensible precaution of purchasing two-way radios in order to keep in touch with their children, who could, of course, be anywhere on this vast ship (although the lifts are usually a good bet). All over the craft, you can see parents (and it's usually fathers) with these toy walkie-talkies (and that's showing my age) clamped to their ear, entirely oblivious to the fact that the apparatus is decorated in Day-Glo orange or Barbie pink. And they're having longer conversations with their offspring than they ever would have face-to-face. Although they're actually trying to find where little Cheyenne and Peyton are at this moment, in their mind's eye they are talking to Red Leader about bandits at six-o-clock, as they barrel over the White Cliffs of Dover.

The last element of the ensemble has to be the reflective sunglasses, by which I mean sunglasses coated with a mirrored surface on the outer surface. I suppose that's a statement of the blindingly obvious - having the mirrored surface on the inside would just give you an up close and personal view of the inside of each eyeball, which would be somewhat disconcerting. Armed with our sunglasses we are suddenly every American motorcycle cop we've ever seen on T.V. Miscreants pale at the image of themselves captured in our lenses and then, for added effect, we can whip the glasses off to pin them down with our steely glare.

There you have it, the ideal present. Cheap, easy to get hold of and guaranteed to deliver unlimited joy on the part of the recipient. You'll thank me for it one of these days but the happiness of my fellow man is thanks enough. Ok chaps, are you receiving, over?

The whole business of present-giving generated this story...

You'd Better Watch Out!

In common with parents up and down the country, Christmas Eve found Wayne Trubshaw busily scrabbling under the Christmas Tree, transferring presents between a sack and the pile around the base.

The difference, in Wayne's case, was that he was transferring the presents to his sack, not from it. Wayne had taken the concept of last-minute Christmas shopping to its logical conclusion. He simply waited for everyone else to do their shopping and was now using the last few hours of darkness, before Christmas Day, to relieve them of it.

Unlike most parents, he didn't have the time, or the inclination, to make considered choices. He just had to hope that whatever had been purchased for the kids who lived in this posh pile, would be more than good enough for little Jaycee and Brad. With luck, there might be a game controller or two, perhaps a tablet, laptop or top-of-the-range mobile phone? Wayne had no time to find out, he had to grab and run. Burglars can't be choosers, he told himself.

Heaving the heavily-laden sack onto his back, Wayne edged gingerly through the furnishing, trying not to make a sound. He headed toward the grey light that signified the patio doors and successful escape. All was going well, until a tremendous flash temporarily blinded him. Taking a tentative step forward, he tripped and fell head-first into the parquet floor with a noise that would wake the dead. As his sight gradually returned, he became aware of a narrow beam of light shining on him from the left. His eyes followed the light to its owner, a small, serious-looking boy, holding a tiny torch and peering at him through a large pair of spectacles. He appeared to be holding one end of a skipping rope.

"Is it him?" a female voice from Wayne's right asked.

"No" replied the boy, with evident disappointment. "I told you it wouldn't be"

Wayne turned his head to the right, with some difficulty as he was lying face down on the floor and was pinned in that position by the weight of the sack on his back. From under a table, in the light of the torch, he could make out the figure of a little girl sitting cross-legged in her nightgown. She appeared to be holding the other end of the skipping rope.

"Oh" she said, sadly, "I felt sure we had him this time" She edged a little closer to Wayne. He could now see the frayed and worn teddy bear clamped under her arm.

"Are you Santa?" She fixed him with an accusatory glare. Glad of any chance to mount a defence, Wayne responded.

"Not exactly" He heard a snort of derision from his left as he thought as fast as he could of a faintly believable explanation. "You know how everything has an opposite, like positive and negative?"

"Good and bad?" suggested the little girl, straying into an area with which Wayne was not entirely comfortable.

"Matter and anti-matter" the voice from the left chipped in.

"I was going to say Liverpool and Everton, but that and all I suppose" Wayne conceded without turning his head. "Well, there's your Santa and then there's your..."

"Anti-Santa?" asked the boy, incredulously.

"Yeah" said Wayne with relief, "that's me"

"What does an Anti-Santa do then?" the little girl asked suspiciously

"Well, you see, Santa brings presents to good children, doesn't he?" Wayne's mind was racing to keep up with his mouth. It was also getting uncomfortably hot under both the weight of the sack and the close observation. The girl nodded slowly in agreement with his statement. "Well, I take them away"

"Why would you do that?" asked the boy, who was getting right on Wayne's nerves.

"To give to poor children who don't have any" Wayne suggested. It seemed a pretty good story, even if he said so himself. It would certainly be true of Jaycee and Brad if he didn't get this load home tonight.

"Presumably, if they don't have presents, then they haven't been good?" The boy pointed out.

"It doesn't always work like that" Wayne snapped.

"What sort of presents were you looking for?" The little girl asked.

"Oh, I don't know" Wayne blustered, "electrical gizmos I suppose, mostly. Game controllers, tablets, that kind of thing"

"We never have things like that" the girl said, sadly. "We get 'good, wholesome and improving' presents" She sounded as if she was quoting someone.

"Pru's right. We never get electronics" the boy agreed, with a voice tinged with disappointment.

"Pru?" Wayne asked.

"Oh, sorry, where are my manners. I'm Peregrine and this is my sister, Prudence"

"Peregrine? Like the bird?"

"There is a raptor of the same nomenclature, yes" Peregrine responded huffily.

"What's your name?" Prudence enquired.

"Wayne" he responded before he could stop himself.

"A Wayne in a manger!" She giggled, and pointed to the floor. Wayne realised that he was surrounded by a sea of small plastic figures, sheep, donkeys and cows. He must have broken his fall on a toy manger.

The digging pain in his chest was probably a wise man, shepherd or the infant Jesus getting his retribution in early.

"Look, do you mind if I sit up now? It's getting a bit hard on this floor" Wayne suggested.

"Please do" responded Peregrine, ever the charming host.

Wayne managed to shuffle into a sitting position whilst still keeping a firm hold on the sack of presents.

"So, what sort of thing do you guys get from Santa?" he decided he might as well know the worst.

"Well, Aunt Wilhelmina always knits us a scarf" Prudence replied, helpfully.

"That's not so bad, is it?" Wayne remarked, affably, "nice warm scarf each, at this time of year?"

"Oh no, not each" Peregrine explained, "She knits us a scarf. Mummy and daddy insist that we wear it when she visits. It's a bit of a bother, really. If we don't co-ordinate our movements exactly, I nearly get strangled, with Prudence being so much shorter"

"You must get other things, surely?"

"I had a year's subscription to New Scientist last year" Peregrine said, cheerfully, "it's a bit populist, but perfectly adequate"

Wayne was beginning to realise that he might have made a huge mistake in his choice of target.

"Bet you have a great Christmas Day though? Groaning table piled with rich food and all that?" If the presents were naff, perhaps he could nick their Christmas Dinner.

"Not really. Do you like nut roast?" Peregrine enquired.

"Never tried it"

"Don't!" Peregrine responded with feeling "it's an acquired taste and I wouldn't bother if I were you"

"Christmas Pudding?" Wayne suggested

"We're only allowed ice cream" Prudence said, sulkily.

"You can get some nice flavours of ice cream these days" Wayne was trying desperately to inject a little Christmas cheer into the conversation, "Pistachio, toffee, mint-choc chip"

"Vanilla" Prudence said, flatly, "Daddy doesn't approve of 'artificial colours and flavourings'" she was clearly quoting again.

"Strewth!" Wayne said, with feeling, "anything would be better than nut roast and vanilla ice cream. Fish and chips even."

"Fish and chips?" Peregrine querled

"Oh, don't tell me you've never had fish and chips?" Wayne asked, appalled.

"Don't think so. What are they like?" Prudence asked, with interest.

"Right, that settles it" Wayne came to a sudden decision, "The Chippy in the arcade round the corner's open late. You two are coming with me for a decent nosh"

Five minutes later, the three of them were sitting around a Formica table in the Paphos Fish Bar, fish and chips piled before them. Wayne had the sack of presents firmly tucked under his chair - after all, waste not, want not. He looked at the two children, busily tucking into the food before them, with a sense of pride. This was the first time he had ever, consciously, done a good deed and he rather liked the feeling it gave him.

"What the dickens are you two doing here?" the authoritative male voice from behind him made Wayne visibly jump a foot in the air.

"Hi dad!" Peregrine responded brightly.

"Dad?" Wayne yelped, with a sinking feeling.

"This is Wayne" Prudence advised, between large mouthfuls of chips, "he's an Anti-Santa"

"And a burglar" Peregrine added, "we've got pictures and the stolen goods are in a bag under his chair"

"Hang on a minute!" Wayne interjected, before the uniformed presence of their father loomed over him.

"Evening, Constable" he said, with a nervous smile.

"We knew Mr. Nicolaides would ring you as soon as we turned up on Christmas Eve with a strange man in tow" Peregrine smiled as he mopped up the remainder of his meal, "So, we caught your burglar, now do we get our i-pads, like you promised?"

By the way, as with most things, whether you believe in Santa Claus, or not, has no effect on his existence...
You'd better not pout, you'd better not cry...

When did you stop believing in Santa Claus?

If you find this question difficult (largely because you were still hanging on to your belief with grim determination) then please stop reading at this point. For the rest of us, I'm willing to bet that this particular moment is ingrained in your memory.

When you consider the elaborate belief systems with which we indoctrinate our children, only for them to discover with each passing year that these firmly held beliefs are groundless, it must say something about the human spirit that we are prepared to believe in anything, ever again. In evidence, I submit The Easter Bunny, The Tooth Fairy and, last but most definitely not least, Father Christmas.

My own particular crisis of faith, with regard to Santa anyway, happened when I was 10 years old on a Saturday night, just before Christmas, 1964.

At the time, we kept a pub. The pub was of an old-fashioned design, in which the living room and kitchen were tucked away behind the serving area, whilst all the other living accommodation (bedrooms and bathroom) were upstairs. In order to get from the living room to the bedrooms, it was necessary to cross The Passage. The Passage was really a corridor to allow access to the Public Bar and Smoke Room but also contained some tables and seating, and our solitary fruit machine. Access across The Passage to the bedrooms was fairly straightforward in the week, when only a small group of hardy customers would be huddled by the serving hatch or by the fruit machine. At weekends, however, The Passage would be crowded with revellers in assorted degrees of intoxication.

The pub was equipped with a woefully inadequate coal-fired boiler that just about managed to heat the public rooms but left the bedrooms as something of an arctic wasteland. Mum therefore insisted that I change for bed in front of the fire in the living room, to avoid frostbite or hypothermia. Unfortunately, this meant crossing The Passage to get to the stairs, now attired in pyjamas, dressing gown and slippers.

During the week, with a little careful timing, I usually managed this largely unnoticed. On a Saturday night however, and particularly at the weekend before Christmas, the only way across was to force my way through the smoke-wreathed throng. This was always acutely embarrassing, and a journey I tried to complete as quickly as possible. On this occasion, however, my rapid transit was thwarted by my youngest uncle suddenly appearing from the crowd at the bottom of the stairs and grabbing my arm.

"I just wanted you to know that I've left your present with your mum for Christmas Day. Thought I ought to tell you. Of course, you don't believe in Santa Claus any more do you?" He laughed.

I muttered my thanks and swallowed hard. In that moment, I didn't believe in Santa Claus, but right up to then I had believed with the sort of dogged fervour that only children can muster. Of course, my compatriots at school had, over the years, come to the conclusion that Santa Claus did not exist but I had hung on to my faith, largely because the alternative didn't seem too inviting and I was keen to keep the magic of Christmas in one form or another. Now, in one sentence, it was gone.

I still miss Santa. Christmas without him has never been the same. But I suppose if anyone is responsible for that curious bonhomie that arises at some point on Christmas Eve and has disappeared without trace by Boxing Day, maybe we should thank the vestige of Father Christmas, and be grateful.

And, regardless of my uncle, I still track Santa on the NORAD website every Christmas Eve, so there!

Back in 2005, when I published my first collection of stories 'Steady Past Your Granny's', I included a story in which I imagined an alternative version of the Nativity, an AlterNativity, in 'A Stable Upbringing'. Ever since then, with each passing Christmas, I've been writing prequels and sequels to it, starting with this...

The Night Watch

It was a clear night. In fact it was a very clear night. Bright points of light peppered the sky, but these paled in comparison with the gigantic 'star' currently appearing to hang over the small village in the valley.

In a field on the hillside, two shepherds sat on a rocky outcrop and regarded the 'star' glumly. Eventually, one turned to the other and said, conversationally,

"I'm sore afraid"

There was a pause, during which his companion digested this news.

"Well, which?" he asked, eventually.

"What do you mean?"

"Well, what I mean is, are you sore? Or are you afraid? Can't be both, don't make any sense that."

"I mean what I say, and I say what I mean." the first shepherd said, glaring at his companion, "I'm sore from sitting on this ruddy rock and I'm afraid that damn great star up there is going to put us out of business." Somewhere in the distance, a wolf howled. "Look," the shepherd continued, warming to his theme, "what's the point in us being here, watching our flocks by night, as it says in the job description..."

"As it says in the job description, agreed." His companion nodded.

"Well, what's the point if it's going to be like daylight all the time? What creature is going to be daft enough to try something in broad daylight?" He eased a weary buttock from the rock beneath and shuffled a little.

"Take your point, comrade, take your point." The second shepherd chewed the idea, along with a length of straw he had been saving for just such an occasion. "So, you are of the view that the aforesaid and alleged 'star' hanging above us, is, in point of fact and notwithstanding, a celestial conspiracy to deprive us of our rightful livelihood, to wit, being a shepherd watching his, or as it may indeed be, her, flock by night?"

The first shepherd squirmed on his rocky repository a little, thought this statement over, gave it due consideration and said, "You what?"

"I said," the second shepherd sighed deeply, "that if this bright light goes on, we'll all be out on our ears. Remember when it turned up?"

"How could I forget?" The first shepherd muttered glumly, "what with that coming out of nowhere and ruddy choral singing belting out in every direction...the effect it had on my sheep"

"Not good?"

"Not good! You know what sheep are like. Scared stiff is how they are when things are fine. Add a blinding bright light, and all that singing, and you've got some seriously terrified sheep. And you know what happens if you frighten a sheep?"

"Yeah." said his companion with feeling.

"It was like a skating rink round here. Took me all my time to stand up without falling over. And, of course, the last thing you wanted to do was fall over. Bloody star!" He said with feeling, "we don't even know what it is."

"Ah now, I may be able to furnish you with a little inside knowledge there," the second shepherd looked around conspiratorially, "You see Earl over there?" he nodded toward the lone silhouette of a shepherd on the horizon. The first shepherd nodded his agreement. "Well, he's been giving it some thought, and he reckons it's a supernova."

The second shepherd folded his arms and attempted to look wise, which unfortunately left him with the appearance of someone experiencing a severe bilious attack.

"A supernova?" The first shepherd thought about

this for a while, and eventually caved in, "what's one of them when it's at home?"

"I thought you might ask that, brother," said the second shepherd, looking somewhat smug, "you know those Brit slaves the Romans brought here?" The first shepherd nodded. "Well, they've got this game, right, where they all stand round in a circle and one chucks a ball at the other, you know what I mean?"

"I've seen 'em at it," the first shepherd confirmed, "It's called Rickets." He said with some pride.

"Rickets? Is it? Well, If you say so." The second shepherd gave his companion a hard stare."Any road, at some point the one chucking the ball gets fed up with it and lets the other one have a go, and that," he said smugly" is called a Nova."

"Says who?"

"Says Earl."

"Oh, right. Well, he would know," the first shepherd conceded, "Earl's a thinker. So, a Nova is a point in the game where they change ends, right?"

"Yeah, that's it." The second shepherd congratulated himself on working his way through a tricky conversation.

"Right." The first shepherd decided to quit while he was ahead. "Here, there's a kid bawling his eyes out down there. We're doing no good here. Let's grab a lamb, go down, and see if we can cadge a cup of tea. Kids

like lambs. We might even get a few bob off the father if we can get him to shut up."

With a lamb under his arm, the second shepherd helped his friend up off the rock and they set off, cautiously, because the sheep were still somewhat anxious, in the direction of the village and the 'star'.

"What's a supernova then?" The first shepherd asked, and immediately regretted it, as they picked their way down the hillside.

"Well, it stands to reason dunnit"

"Does it?"

"Yeah, course it does. If a Nova is the time where the game changes a bit, then a Supernova must be...must be..."

"Oh, I'm with you." The first shepherd stopped to catch his breath and looked up at the 'star'. "It must be where the game changes completely!"

"That's it" said the second shepherd with some relief, "it's a game-changing event, that's what it is."

Lessons from Carols

Regular readers of these ramblings of mine (if there are such people) would be forgiven for asking, "Well, was there anything you were good at?" particularly after my previous revelations of my shortcomings in woodwork and technical drawing. The answer, despite the evidence of these articles, is, yes, English. In all my years at Anglesey Secondary Modern, this was the only lesson in which I regularly came top, or next to top, of the class. The 'next to top' bit came about because I was locked in a battle for supremacy with Kathryn McG. for the English crown and, to be fair, she was considerably prettier than I was.

Being good at something was a rare treat for me and you might have thought, given my other failings, that I would have tempered my success with a degree of humility? Not a bit of it! I became arrogant. This was particularly apparent during those sessions when each member of the class had to read aloud a section of whichever tome we were exploring at the time. Some of the class could read really well, with the correct intonation, inflection and phrasing, but they were in the minority. We had quite a number of the "I'm alright as long as I keep my finger following each word" brigade, whose intense concentration on figuring out what it was that they were reading, wrecked any chance of adding anything other than a dull monotone to the recitation. Reading a book at this pedestrian rate used to drive me mad, so I would often have jumped ahead by a chapter or two whilst I was waiting, which caused problems when it came to my turn and I realised I had no idea where we had got up to.

Being able to read effectively, and with something other than a drone, meant that I was often pressed into service to read a lesson or similar at Assembly. As a consequence, I was even more likely to be dragooned into the cast for the Christmas Carol Service, which the school held at our local church, All Saints' in Branston Road. I don't know whether it was because they felt I could handle difficult words and phrases or because they had me down as a boring little tyke with no sense of the dramatic, but I never, ever, got the interesting lessons with the dramatic announcements, such as "Unto us a child is born..."Isaiah 9:6. No, I always got the somewhat dense and impenetrable "In the beginning was the word, and the word was with God..." etc., from John 1:1. Standing at the lectern, declaiming these words, I was acutely aware of the congregation shifting in their seats as they waited for the interesting Nativity stuff to start.

Carols used to pose a problem for the reluctant readers, and for me too. For example, that well known line "Lo, he abhors not the virgin's womb" from "Hark! The Herald Angels Sing". Firstly, the term 'virgin' always caused a deal of unnecessary sniggering in the ranks because, even though some words might have baffled us, that one didn't and if we weren't exactly sure what it meant, we knew it was risqué.

"Womb" however, was another matter (you have to remember that this was the early 1960s and we were pretty naïve). Firstly, we had to figure out how to pronounce it. I could usually make a fairly accurate guess, based on the rhyming scheme of the hymn, but this had me foxed. You may recall that this line follows that other impenetrable phrase "Late in time, behold him come" which defied any interpretation. So, if the rhyming word is "come" (and remember we're talking about Burtonian pronunciation here), then that would make 'womb' - "Wum", as in 'Mum', which didn't seem likely. Eventually, I settled on 'womb' as in 'bomb', which seemed vaguely logical, but had me perplexed. I couldn't see how a truncated Womble fitted into the Nativity.

I must have sung ""Hark! The Herald Angels Sing" on countless occasions over the years, and each time I have this uncontrollable urge to get the pronunciation wrong, just for old time's sake.

Sing a Song of Christmas

Christmas is a time for singing, even for the tone deaf amongst us, and two memories of very different Christmas songs from the mid-1960s, came to my mind. The first involved me as a chorister at All Saint's Church in Branston Road.

It was a tradition at Christmas that the Church Choir, or as much of it as could be mustered, would take a tour of the local pubs for a spot of carol singing. The purpose of this was to reach out to the community, particularly that section of it that preferred the pub to the pulpit, and to raise some welcome funds from the collection. I also rather suspect that the adult choristers (all men, it was very much a male bastion) were quite keen on what was, in essence, an officially sanctioned pub crawl.

I used to find the whole experience somewhat embarrassing. It was bad enough that we had to wear the full chorister outfit of cassock, surplice and ruff in church, outside it looked decidedly odd. The redeeming feature for all of the boys in the choir was that we were given a modest sum for our efforts. I think the going rate was half a crown, which bought quite a lot in those days.

Our tour usually included The Blackpool Inn, The Branston Arms and The New Talbot, and possibly The Cooper's Arms and The Argyle Arms. Once inside the pub, coats were removed and we were exposed in our garb to some sniggering and muted cat-calls from the usually crowded pubs. The juke box or background music would be stilled and we would launch into a quick burst of some favourite carols, followed by the collection plate being passed around.

My problem was that I was quite well known in the local pubs, not only because I was the son of a landlord but also as a frequent, if rather reluctant, companion to my dad whenever he pottered out to 'check out the competition'. Therefore, I was frequently assailed with cries of "Hey up, Pip! How yer doing?" whilst I tried to look angelic and spiritual.

This problem reached a peak, of course, when we visited The New Talbot, where I was very well known indeed. I would be crimson with embarrassment as we went through our set list of songs, knowing full well that I was the focus of attention of much of the room, not to mention my mum and dad

The second memory has to do with our first Christmas at The New Talbot. We had moved in to the pub in late autumn and had enjoyed the early rush of customers keen to see the new landlord and landlady. The question was, whether that initial surge of interest could be sustained? Thankfully, it was.

My mum and dad were relatively young for the pub trade at that time (early 40s) and were seen as a breath of fresh air with their friendly, relaxed and convivial approach. Dad had also learned the art of keeping cask-conditioned ale, from his years of serving at The Branston Arms and The Labourers Union. Keeping a good pint was critical to success, particularly in the 1960s when cask ale was notoriously temperamental and needed careful nurturing.

When Christmas approached, we anticipated a very busy period indeed. Dad had placed a significant order with the brewery and, one night before Christmas, he insisted that I should come down into the cellar with him.

There, on the thralls, the hogsheads of beer were lined up, all busily working away at their secondary fermentation. It was unusual to have hogsheads, as these contain 1½ barrels and you had to be pretty certain that you would sell that amount. To have a cellar full of them showed confidence indeed.

As the fermentation process took place, the casks would whistle a little as the excess gases escaped through the pegs. A whole cellar full, therefore, created quite a cacophony.

"Listen to them, Pip" my dad said, his eyes glistening with emotion, "they're singing!"

And, do you know, I rather think they were.

You know those rather annoying, relentlessly positive and rather boastful, 'round robin' letters that accompany some Christmas cards? Well, I decided to take the idea to its logical extreme...

<u>Yuletide Greetings from the Smith's!</u>

Dear All,

Well, who would have guessed it, Christmas time again! Where does the year go to?

As always, the Smith family have had a very full year indeed!

It all started brilliantly, with the Board of Roland's company finally seeing sense and promoting him to CFO (whatever that is!) It was such a shame that all of that 'insider' dealing nonsense took some of the shine off his success, but, as I said to him, if you must deal at all I would rather you did it inside, where it's nice and warm!

I think it's a testament to the Company, and to Roland, that they've agreed he should spend a lot more time with his family, pursuing other projects, as the Company announcement to the City put it.

I think it's an open secret now that Tamsin was shortlisted for a Nobel Prize this year and missed out, by a whisker, to the Dalai Lama (again!) She left for the Northern Tribal region of Pakistan a few days ago to do some missionary work for our local church. Our vicar, Mohammed (yes, we were surprised too!) is really charismatic and certainly has Tamsin under his spell. He says that she'll meet a lot of really, salt-of-the-earth, local chaps who will be just itching to convert to Christianity and he's sure a female missionary will go down a storm. We haven't heard from her yet but we're sure she'll be just fine.

Algernon managed 5 A*, 2 As and a B in his exams. We were a bit disappointed with the B grade but, as he rightly pointed out, it is hard reading Braille with a hook. Utter nonsense, of course, he has a perfectly good, state-of-the-art, prosthesis, if he chooses to wear it, but he can never resist his little joke! He's going to spend the hols climbing Everest with a bunch of pals, without the aid of oxygen! Just hope he's going to be able to hold his breath for that long (LOL).

As usual, we have had some really interesting and unusual holidays this year. Roland said we should concentrate on places without an extradition treaty (he's such a hoot!)

We started with spring in Afghanistan. Very hot with some great cuisine, but a little restrictive. Topless sunbathing turned out not to be the done thing and any adolescent high-jinks, such as shoplifting, were very much frowned upon (hence Algernon's prosthesis). Guantanamo Bay sounded like such a romantic spot for our summer holiday, and the weather was lovely, but all of the locals sported full beards, and orange jumpsuits seemed to be de rigeur, which didn't work well if you fancied an all over tan (ROTFL - whatever that means!) North Korea, in the autumn, was surprisingly friendly, amazingly cheap and we had a great time. In fact, Roland is still there at the time of writing, pursuing some internet-based business opportunity, or other. He assures me that it should all be over by Christmas!

Well, I must dash and get on with all of the Christmassy things I've been putting off by writing this letter! With Tamsin, Algernon and Roland all away, I'm rather rattling around Smith Hall at present. Of course, I do have dear old Richter, our faithful Rottweiler, to look after me.

Richter and I get along famously, but he's always been more Roland's dog than mine and he has taken to knocking me to the floor and shaking me, which can be a bit irritating, but I'm sure we'll manage to rub along until his 'master' returns.

Hope you all have a lovely Christmas and a splendid New Year. I'm sure we'll have lots to tell you next time ⍰

The Smith Family x

Crackers at Christmas

When I wrote this, I was on what is alliteratively known as a 'Turkey and Tinsel' break. This was not intentional. We booked this weekend as a base for visiting some friends, only to find that Christmas had broken out all around us. Apparently, this type of break starts at the beginning of November and continues up to and including the real thing.

This format can be a bit disconcerting. Friday, for instance, was designated as Christmas Eve, Saturday was Christmas Day and, in a fit of time compression that would delight British Industry, Sunday is New Year's Eve. This rather conveniently disposes of the seasonal festivities in one fell swoop but I should think the staff will be about at screaming pitch come the festive season proper.

All of this made me think of Christmas Past, when things were nowhere near as well organised. An example of this was when we kept The New Talbot Hotel in Anglesey Road in the mid-1960s. We had been invited to Christmas Dinner at my aunt and uncle's. Dad insisted on providing the turkey for this feast, which was something of a concern because dad disliked doing anything in a conventional manner. If he bought anything, it was always through 'someone who knows someone' who could get it cheaper, bigger or faster (or all three). This sort of arrangement tended to lead to considerable uncertainty, which was not conducive to the peace of mind of my aunt and uncle, who were great ones for doing things properly. Thus the scene was set for potential disaster.

As the days before Christmas gradually diminished, my aunt made repeated requests to know what size of bird to expect, but was always fobbed off by dad (who probably didn't know the answer himself).

Christmas Eve arrived and, as good as his word, dad delivered a fresh turkey, albeit rather late in the day. However, in a fit of generosity (probably brought on by the fact that Christmas Eve was dad's birthday, which he did like to celebrate) he had bought something that resembled a small ostrich.

My aunt had a relatively small kitchen and there really wasn't enough room in there for her and this bird. The problem was compounded on Christmas Morning, when, having prepared this avian monster for the oven (a not inconsiderable feat) it became apparent that it would not fit into the oven. Only savage butchery reduced the beast to portions that could realistically be prised in. Even then, the sheer size of the fowl led to the generation of so much fat that the kitchen looked like the morning after a riot in a chip shop.

The whole thing took much longer to cook than normal and the eventual result, despite my aunt's acknowledged culinary skills, was not up to her usual high standards. She was left quivering on the edge of either murdering my dad or having a nervous breakdown, whichever was the easier. Typically, dad couldn't see what all the fuss was about and was somewhat miffed not to be the hero of the hour.

Dad (on left of barrels) with a few like-minded friends

Another occasion when things didn't go particularly well was Christmas, 1973. This was my first Christmas with a girlfriend in evidence (I was something of a late starter). We were not spending Christmas Day together, so she had given me a present to open on the day. I was a bit wary of opening this at home as mum didn't exactly approve of my girlfriend. Come the day and, after diplomatically opening the presents from my parents and my sister, I eagerly set about unwrapping my girlfriend's gift.

It was a jumper. It was a very colourful jumper. In fact, it looked how I imagine a migraine might feel. Better still, it was figure hugging. This would have been fine, had I possessed a figure worth hugging.

Unfortunately, my physique over the years has transformed from painfully emaciated to borderline obese without ever passing through any of the more appealing stages in between. At this time, I was in the former category. To complete the effect, the sleeves were too short for my arms, leaving 6 inches or so of thin wrist and forearm fetchingly peeping out. Mum and my sister fell about laughing when I tried it on, leaving me cringing with embarrassment but absolutely adamant that I loved it.

On Boxing Day, sporting my new jumper under my favourite PVC imitation leather jacket (the 1970s were not a good time for fashion) I met my girlfriend. When I took my jacket off, she too fell about laughing. It wasn't a long-lasting relationship.

The PVC jacket when I was a few years younger,
with Auntie Vera and Uncle Jim in the background

The King Thing

It had been a long and arduous journey. Long, because any journey, where you're not really sure where you're going, is bound to be perceived as long. Arduous because they were travelling on camels, and there is nothing more arduous than a camel, especially when you are not really used to camels...or travelling for that matter. But now, they dared to hope that their journey was almost completed. The star that they had been 'following', hung brightly before them and seemed to indicate, as far as a star could indicate anything, that the location they were searching for was just below them.

From the rear of the party, there came a timeless and familiar cry.

"Are we there yet?"

"No, we are not, Melchior, and that is the three hundred and fourteenth time you have asked me that since we set out" Balthazar fumed.

"Alright, alright, keep your crown on dear, just asking" Melchior muttered.

"There's some men walking on the road ahead" Caspar pointed out, "perhaps they might know where we can find him?"

"Ah yes, honest shepherds" Balthazar noted with

satisfaction, "just the chaps to have the local knowledge we're looking for. Leave this to me." As his camel drew level with the shepherds, he drew himself up to his full height and leaned forward (which is not easy to do on a camel). Adopting his best 'talking to foreign peasants' accent, he thundered "LO!"

The first shepherd jumped a couple of feet in the air, and the second quickly hid behind him. Rapidly recovering his composure, the first shepherd looked up at the richly dressed man looming above him, crown sparkling in the starlight. He looked back at his companion, jerking his head in the direction of the king, in the time-honoured fashion that has meant "We've got a right one here" down the ages.

"Of course we're 'low' to you, comrade, sitting up there, lording it over us on your camel, whilst we honest artisans are down here with the sheep"

"What did he say?" asked Melchior

"Something about lard, sheep and I think he's called Honest Artie Sans" Caspar hazarded a guess based on his limited knowledge of foreign tongues.

"Ah, a bookmaker!" Melchior noted with satisfaction, "See what odds he's offering on the sex of the baby"

Balthazar, whose knowledge of the local language was somewhat better than his compatriots, ignored their babble and bent to his task.

"WE SEARCH FOR A KING" He bellowed

"What did he say?" asked the second shepherd

"He said they're searching for aching" the first shepherd said with an air of authority

"Shouldn't think they would need to search far, on the back of those things" the second shepherd noted, "I doubt they'll be able to sit down for a fortnight"

"What do you want from us?" the first shepherd reasonably asked

"WE NEED TO KNOW, oh the hell with this, I'll come down" Balthazar gave a shouted command to his camel, which duly ignored him but Melchior's promptly sank to its knees, depositing him unceremoniously on the ground.

"You git, Balthazar!" He yelled as he dusted the sand from his raiments, "that's the third time you've played that trick"

"Sorry about that, old chap" Balthazar apologised, "it's just a matter of getting the inflection right." He tried again, and this time his camel sank to its knees. Regrettably, Melchior's simultaneously sprang up just as he was about to remount, causing him to tumble backwards onto a pile of sheep droppings.

"Now then, as I was saying" Balthazar said to the first shepherd "we are searching for a child"

"We? How many are you?" the first shepherd asked. He had been trying to work this out since they first arrived. Each time he looked, it seemed as if there were a different number of camels and riders, sometimes more, sometimes less.

"Ah, that is indefinite" Balthazar said enigmatically

"Indefinite? What do you mean, 'indefinite'? You must know how many there are of you?"

"Not at all." Balthazar insisted, "It is not written in The Book, therefore, we are indefinite."

"Have you tried c...c...counting?" the second shepherd asked. The whole unsettling experience had brought back his childhood stutter.

"We can't" Balthazar said smugly "we think it's quantum"

"Really?" Observed the second shepherd, "I h...h...had the same problem but I just thought it was because I was th...th...thick"

"Quantum? What the hell's quantum when it's at home?" asked the first shepherd, trying to take command of the conversation again.

"Ah well," Balthazar smoothed his beard in a manner that was intended to denote great wisdom, but which only succeeded in adding a good number of camel hairs to his own collection, "in this case, quantum means a situation in which the action of observing something affects the outcome."

"Getaway!" the first shepherd said, disparagingly

"Pull the other one, it's got b...b...bells on it" the second shepherd averred with enthusiasm

"What's got bells on it?" the first shepherd enquired

"I d...d...dunno" the second shepherd was forced to admit, "It was something my old mum used to say."

"And did hers have bells on it?"

"Oh yes, she was a b...b...belly dancer."

None of this exchange had meant anything at all to Balthazar, but he felt he should try to educate these peasants before he went on his way. Noblesse oblige and all that.

"Look, it's like you and your sheep. When you count them, does it always come to the same number?"

"Well, no." the first shepherd admitted, "then again, I fall asleep more often than not when I'm counting and lose track."

"There you are then, that's quantum." Balthazar said with some satisfaction, "you have an indefinite number of sheep"

"I do not have an indefinite number of sheep!" The first shepherd shouted, with feeling "I have 356 sheep, I'll have you know. It just doesn't always work out to that number when I count them."

"Quantum!" Balthazar said triumphantly

"Is that the s..s..same as the w..w..wolf having them?" The second shepherd asked.

"Must be." The first shepherd agreed, "Wouldn't have thought they would have been bold enough to scoff a few kings though"

"To return to my original point" Balthazar said firmly, "Do you know where the royal child is to be found?"

"You reckon there's a royal kid around here somewhere?"

"P...p...pull the other one..."the second shepherd began, and then thought better of it

"Doesn't really seem very likely, does it squire?" the first shepherd pointed out, "All there is here is sheep as far as the eye can see, and that bit of a town. Granted, there's a kid screaming blue murder down there, but it stands to reason it ain't gonna be royalty don't it? Have you tried Herod?"

"What is 'Herod'?" Balthazar asked, half expecting to be told it was a type of embrocation, which, on reflection, he thought, wouldn't be a bad thing.

"Roman b...b...bastard" the second shepherd said with feeling, "Oh, b...b...begging Your Grace's pardon" he went to tug a forelock but realised he didn't know what one was.

"Don't be abasing yourself in front of him, brother" the first shepherd said swiftly, "Just 'cause he's turned up with an indefinite number of mates riding camels, doesn't make him no better than you and me"

"Balthy, sweetheart, are we there yet?" Melchior pleaded

"Belt up, Melchior, or I'll make your camel go down on you again" Balthazar snapped.

"Ooh, saucy!" Melchior pouted, "See, I told you he was doing it deliberately" He muttered to Caspar.

"Now," said Balthazar with more patience than he was actually feeling, "what is 'Herod'?"

"Reckons he's King around here" the first shepherd admitted, "I didn't vote for him though. Would have thought he was past it for knocking out nippers, but you never know."

"Then he must be our goal." Balthazar argued confidently, "Where shall we find him?"

"A few miles that way." the first shepherd pointed to the West," Ruddy great palace, you can't miss it"

"That way? Are you sure? Only the horoscope we drew up distinctly said..."

"Oh, horoscope is it?" the first shepherd asked with interest, "What did it say about him then?"

"The child?" Balthazar asked distractedly, "Well, he's a Capricorn"

"S..s..same as me!" The second shepherd said excitedly

"Can you do mine?" The first shepherd asked

"Yes," said Balthazar, climbing unsteadily onto his camel, "You're in for a big surprise."

"Same old tripe they always come up with" the first shepherd muttered disappointedly as an indeterminate number of camels and kings loped into the distance, "you an' all!" he shouted after them.

"Wer..Wer..What do you mean by that?"

"Werl, I can't see Herod being too chuffed when a load of foreign types turn up at his gaff asking to see a new king, can you?"

They walked on, chuckling to themselves.

"You don't think..." the second shepherd began, hesitantly

"What's that, comrade?"

"You don't think this baby down here could be...?"

"This king you mean?" The first shepherd reflected for a moment, "who knows? Got as much right as anyone else, I suppose"

"I was just thinking, you know...a lamb! Doesn't seem much does it?"

"It does to a ewe! Anyway, don't look at me, brother. All I've got is 2 shekels and a packet of fag papers. You should have tapped that lot up for a tip if you wanted to bring anything else. Crack on it's this year's must-have toy and we've chucked the batteries in too. They'll love it!"

Time, Ye Merry Gentlemen, Please!

Anyone who knew my dad would agree that he liked a drink as much as the next man. Of course, if the next man was an ardent teetotaller, then he liked a drink considerably more. However, as much as he enjoyed a pint (and he did), I believe his real passion was for pub culture.

For some, the average pub is a noisy, smelly place to be visited sparingly, on high days and holidays, for others it is a place in which to consume the maximum possible alcohol within a given period of time, and for yet others it is a second home, a place of fellowship, conviviality and security. My dad belonged to the latter category.

For an illustration of pub culture as it was, take Sunday lunchtimes in the 1960s. Attendance in the pub was viewed by generations of men as sacrosanct. Even those who never went near the place all week could be found in the Public Bar each Sunday between 12.00 until 2.00, as it was then.

When we kept a pub, in Anglesey Road, it used to be my job to open the big double doors to the Public Bar. This happened on the stroke of 12.00, with the pips from the radio fading into the distance and the first chords of "With a Song in my Heart" swelling up to announce the start of Two-way Family Favourites with Cliff Michelmore and Jean Metcalfe (remember that?). Five minutes before this, I would glance out of the window - not a soul to be seen anywhere. Yet, when I opened the doors, I stood a good chance of being killed by a veritable stampede of men hell-bent on their Sunday pint. I used to wonder if they came up through the drains. Within minutes, everyone would be settled in their usual spot. Domino and Card Schools would commence their noisy competition, whilst others bemoaned the fate of their respective football teams the day before (or crowed over the fate of their rivals).

Christmas Day was a sort of substitute Sunday for pub-goers, except that the opening hours were (if memory serves me correctly) even more restricted, to something like an hour at lunchtime and not at all in the evening. The tradition was that, at the pub where you were a 'regular', you would be supplied with your first drink free. The landlord usually guarded this right jealously and would make complicated, and entirely arbitrary, judgements about whether you qualified as a 'regular' or not. Dad was very keen to make sure he got his free pint, so after a whirlwind tour of relatives on Christmas morning; we would head off at a gallop to whichever he deemed to be his current 'local'

Christmas lunchtime in the pub had much the same clientele as Sunday's, and the same 'schools'. The main difference was the general fug of the place, usually cigarette smoke but, on this one day, with more than a little cigar mixed in. Cigars were pretty much a rarity then, except at Christmas. Everyone would feel honour-bound to puff away at their Will's Whiff, Hamlet or Mannekin, gifted by some obscure relative, only to revert gladly to a Park Drive or Woodbine from one of those packs, the size of modern-day laptops, which only appeared at Christmas

Christmas Day nights, however, were my dad's bete noire. The pubs were shut! But, if you were really well-in with your local landlord, you might just be able to get an invite to a 'lock-in' (where the doors had never been unlocked in the first place). This would involve dad "taking the dog for a walk". Over the years we must have had a selection of the fittest dogs in the country. On one memorable occasion this involved a four mile round-trip to Derby Road from South Broadway Street. Dad took his Christmas pub-going really seriously.

I don't think 'pub culture' is what it once was. Now, you're more likely to be served Festive Fayre than make up a four at dominoes.

In an effort to bring my memories of Christmas Day lunchtimes spent in a pub to life, I came up with this...

<u>The Spirit of Christmas</u>

It was 12.05 on 25th December, 1964 and an elderly man dithered outside the corner entrance of a pub, apparently trying to decide whether to enter, or not. 'I know the missus will kill me if I'm late. I've been out all night, after all, but just once it would be nice to...just once' He thought.

The decision was made for him as a whole bunch of people swept into the pub and, more or less, carried him bodily along. Within a few moments, he found himself among the press of bodies by the bar counter. One of the barmaids came over to serve him.

"What can I get you love?" She asked distractedly, eyeing the queue of people waiting to be served.

"Well, I don't really know." He looked around at the other drinkers for inspiration." A pint, I suppose?"

"What do you want, Bitter or Mild?"

"Mild?"

"It's Mercian Mild"

"Mercy and mild?" He mused, "Sounds like something from a carol. I'll try that."

"Are you a regular, love?"

"Am I irregular?" He asked with alarm

"'Cause he ain't" Came a voice from beside him, "he goes at 8.00 every morning, just like clockwork...trouble is...he don't get up until half past!" This sally was followed by a considerable amount of wheezing and guffawing from the middle-aged joke-teller and some dutiful chuckling from those in the immediate vicinity.

"Give over, Ray!" The barmaid shouted, good-naturedly, "You know what I was saying. 'Ere, Jim" She shouted to the Landlord and then mouthed 'Is he a regular?'

"I don't know" Jim peered in the direction of the old man, "he looks familiar. Oh, give him a drink, it's Christmas after all"

"There you go, sweetheart" She handed over a pint of brown-black liquid with a faint head on it, "on the house"

"Oh, thank you!" He ceased rummaging through his pockets and took a sip of the liquid.

"Old Jim always reckons to give his regulars a drink at Christmas. Probably explains why it's so full. I'm Ray, by the way." The joke-teller introduced himself, "this is my brother, Kev"

A slightly younger version of Ray appeared on the old man's right.

"Whiff?" Kev asked.

"Is there?" The old man asked with some embarrassment, "I'm so sorry, I've just finished my shift and I work with animals quite a bit"

"No, no, I meant do you want one of these?" The old man realised that Kev was proffering a shallow tin containing some of the smallest cigars he had ever seen.

"Oh, I see. I don't actually sm..." He began.

"Oh, go on, it's Christmas." The old man reflected on how this seemed to be the rationale for everything, but selected one of the cigars anyway.

"I don't normally smoke myself, but Christmas is different, isn't it? I always get a packet of these" Kev proffered a light and the two began to add considerably to the fug that already filled the bar. The old man coughed enthusiastically for a few minutes.

"If you'd prefer a fag, you can have one of these" Ray offered generously, producing a huge cardboard packet, like an over-sized cigarette pack, from the voluminous pocket of his overcoat. "Christmas present" he explained, "Help yourself, there's a hundred in there"

"It's very kind of you, but I think I'll give it a miss. I've still got this" The old man nodded toward the miniature cigar.

"Have one for Ron" Ray urged.

"Ron?" The old man asked.

"Yeah, later on!" This caused more wheezing and dutiful chuckling.

The old man extracted a cigarette and diplomatically placed it behind his ear.

"I didn't think the place would be so full, it's only just past midday after all" He mused.

"Well, there's the free pint but, on top of that, we've only got an hour before they shut" Ray explained, "and they're not open tonight, either, unless you know where to go." Ray tapped the side of his nose conspiratorially.

"That won't be a problem; I'm only here for an hour or so at the most." The old man confided. He took another sip of his drink and looked at it suspiciously.

"You all right with that?" Kev asked, "I wouldn't touch Mild myself, they can put all sorts in Mild and you'd never know. Can't see through it, can you?"

"I always stick with Bitter. You know where you are with Bitter." Ray agreed, "Of course, there's always that, if you're up for it" He nodded toward a small wooden cask on top of the bar counter.

"What's that? I don't think I've ever seen a cask so small" The old man remarked.

"Pin of Barley Wine. Jim always has one in for Christmas. The deal is that, if you can drink five pints, you get the sixth one free" Ray explained.

"Is that difficult?"

"Put it like this, I like a drink but I couldn't do it. It's very strong. Be like drinking a pint of sherry."

The old man shuddered involuntarily.

"I'm not a big fan of sherry" He told them.

"'Course you're not. Who is? Maiden aunts and vicars. Now, when it comes to the Barley Wine challenge, Matty there's done it twice" Ray said, admiringly.

Matty stood a little further up the bar, clinging on to the counter with a grim purpose and swaying gently. There were several pints of Barley Wine in front of him.

"You alright, Matty?" Ray shouted above the hubbub.

"Yep" "Matty responded, thickly, and inaccurately, "you jusht min' my gerbil.

"Gerbil?" The old man queried.

"There's no gerbil" Ray whispered, "It's just his fancy. If you drank as much Barley Wine as he does, you'd be seeing gerbils an' all. He's a grand bloke but it's a pity for his wife and kids"

After that, somehow the old man found himself embroiled in a game of dominoes, despite admitting that he had never played before. Further pints of Mild were consumed, the taste of which seemed to get better with each one.

"You said you'd just finished your shift" Ray said to him, over the clatter of shuffled dominoes, "d'you work nights then?"

"Sometimes" The old man admitted

"It's a killer of a shift is nights" Ray sympathised.

"I don't mind it, actually" The old man countered, "It isn't every night, and I get a lot of pleasure from my work"

"Yeah, but working at Christmas is no joke, is it?" Kev pointed out.

"You like Christmas, do you?" The old man asked.

"Well, it's for the kids really, isn't it? Santa and all that" Ray said, picking up his dominoes and eyeing them speculatively through a cloud of cigarette smoke.

"You're not a believer then?" The old man enquired.

"I wouldn't say that. I try to get to the Midnight Communion if I can." Ray responded.

"No, I meant about Father Christmas!" The old man chuckled. Ray exploded in laughter, showering cigarette ash in all directions.

"Believe in Santa!" He wheezed, "You're a caution, you are"

"Never found a present and not known where it came from, then?" The old man mused.

"Well, yes of course. The kids are on them like a pack

of wild animals, there's gift wrap and tags flying in all directions. It takes us most of the day to try and piece together who bought what. You're bound to finish up with something where nobody knows who bought it. Stands to reason." Kev pointed out, placing a double-four down with the cryptic comment "Hartshorne Church".

"Ah, I see" The old man studied his dominoes and placed a four-six down, which rather surprised Kev, as he felt sure that he had had that domino in his hand just a moment ago.

Despite the old man's best efforts, no-one would allow him to buy a drink. Not even when a round of shorts was called for as the Landlord rang for Last Orders.

Sentimental Christmas songs were sung with much gusto, led by Ray using a matchbox for percussion, followed by a few popular carols which caused the odd tear to flow down even the grimmest countenance, including the now semi-comatose face of Matty.

The old man noticed that there were very few women present. The odd one popped in to show willing, but they always seemed distracted, as if they were wondering if the turkey was being cremated and if the kids and the dog had demolished the Christmas Tree yet.

Finally, they were all staggering out into the back yard and heading for home.

"Well, the turkey calls" Ray took a deep breath of the fresh Christmas air and momentarily had to prop himself up by the wall of the Gents toilet. "Here's my hand, and here's my heart" He said, emotionally, pumping the old man's hand. "'Ere, I never caught your name"

"Um, it's Nicholas. Just call me Nick" The old man replied.

"Said you work with animals, didn't you? You should get a job with one of the Department Stores - whiskers like that, you'd make a perfect Santa Claus" Kev suggested.

"He would, wouldn't he?" Ray agreed, "Wouldn't surprise me if he'd got a few reindeer out the back there!" He laughed. "Come back and have a drink with us. The wife and kids would love to see you"

"I'd like to but I've got to get back or my wife will kill me." Nick beamed, "but thanks for the invitation. I'll try and drop in on you, sometime"

They said their goodbyes. Ray and Kev made their way unsteadily down the street, whilst Nick doubled back on the pretence of nipping to the Gents, and headed toward the neglected beer garden at the back of the pub.

"Reindeer, indeed!" He muttered, as he fought his way through the brambles. "As if!"

He parted some of the overgrown weeds to reveal a bunch of large kangaroos calmly grazing.

"If they knew anything about Christmas they'd know I use kangaroos every other year, just to keep the antipodeans happy" Nick muttered to himself as he climbed into the sleigh.

A few minutes later, Matty , weaving his way back home, stared blankly upward to try to find out where the cry of Merry Christmas, Matty! had come from.

Above him, framed against the darkening sky, he saw a sleigh being pulled by six snowy white 'boomers', with the old bloke from the pub leaning out and waving. He nearly fell backwards. The gerbil fell off his shoulder!

"Righ'" He said thickly, "Tha' doesh it. No more booze for me."

In the sky above, Nick congratulated himself on this additional Christmas present for Matty's wife and children, and considered how he was going to explain himself when he got back home. 'Oh well' he thought, 'it is Christmas, after all'.

Meanwhile, back at the 'AlterNativity'...

A Room at the Inn

Old Jim sat at the bar, in the grandly named 'House of David' Inn, and stared morosely into his earthenware pot. The room was empty, apart from a couple of shepherds in the corner squabbling over whose round it was. Jim wasn't particularly old, even by the standards of Roman-occupied Bethlehem, but he looked it. Nor, for that matter, was his name Jim, his mother (who really was old) knew him as Jeremiah.

Jim's morose demeanour had a lot to do with the level of liquid in his pot, which at the moment was practically non-existent, coupled with the lack of anyone behind the bar to do anything about it. Just then a curtain at the back of the bar was dragged to one side and Dave, the eponymous Innkeeper, arrived, coughing and spluttering.

"Ruddy hay'll be the death of me!" He wheezed as he poured himself a large pot of wine from an urn.

"What you doin' muckin' around with hay for at this time of night? Ere, gerrus one of those an' all while you're there" Jim grabbed his chance, you never knew when Dave was going to vanish again.

"Just had a couple book in, enni?" Dave coughed

"Are you beddin' em down in hay these days then?" Jim asked in surprise.

"Had to with these two, they wanted the stable, didn't they? I wasn't gonna say no with rooms at the price they're fetching at the moment"

"It's the Romans I blame. Herod!" Jim spat on the sawdust floor with feeling, "couldn't run a kiddies' playground that bloke"

"Shurrup, Jim, you'll gerrus all in trouble" Dave hissed as he looked around the bar, anxiously.

"Gerraway with you, they're not gonna hang around 'ere are they, not yer Romans" Jim chuckled into his pot, "I mean, if you must count everybody, and mark my words it'll only mean more tax for the likes of us" He took a deep draught and wiped his mouth with the back of his hand, "Like I say, if you must count everybody, you'd leave them where they were, wunt you? Not have everyone upping sticks and going back to where they were born?"

"Well, you're still 'ere aren't you?" Dave pointed out "Born 'ere, wunt I. Like my father afore me an' his father afore 'im"

"I didn't think you knew who your father was?"

"Well, 'e must 'ave been from round 'ere, mun't 'e? Mam's never been outside the village in 'er life, an' we don't usually get no visitors, so it stands to reason, dunnit?" Jim said with some feeling. "Any road, just imagine if I said to my goats, 'Now, look 'ere goats. I wanter count yer, but I'm not going to count yer ere, I'm gonna send yer back to the blokes what I bought yer from, an' they can count yer.

Folks'd think I'm barmy!"

"'Course they would. You'd have been talkin' to yer goats for a kick off" Dave pointed out, reasonably.

Jim gave him a hard stare. "You can't move on the roads for folks wanderin' in all directions. How are yer goin' to count 'em when yer don't know where they are anymore, that's what I wanter know?"

The sound of a baby crying lustily, echoed around the yard behind the inn.

"Oh 'eck" Dave slammed his pot down on the bar, "I told 'em I'd get 'em some hot water and towels and now I've forgotten 'cause of you and yer grumbling"

"What they want hot water an' towels for then?"

"Wash the bab with, I guess. She's not long had it, you know" Dave confided.

Dave vanished into a back room. The shepherds continued to bicker in the corner and Jim took another hefty swig from his pot. Dave returned, wiping his hands and inspecting the soles of his shoes.

"Well, that's them sorted, at least for now" He said, moodily wiping something indescribable off his foot. "Any road, it's nice and warm where they are, what with the ox and the ass an' all"

"Yer've never left them animals in there, 'ave yer?" Jim spluttered.

"Where else am I gonna put 'em?" Dave asked,

defensively. "There ain't anywhere. Any road, it'll be summat for the nipper to look at."

Jim shook his head in disbelief. "I'm off round the back to see a man about a donkey"

"See a man about a...? Oh, right, mind your step, it's slippy round there" Dave set to work piling pots back on the shelf.

"Gerrus another an' mind me pot while I'm gone will yer? I dunner trust them two" Jim nodded in the direction of the shepherds, who were now arm-wrestling to decide who should be buying the drinks.

Dave busied himself pouring Jim's wine, trying to ignore the cries of a new-born being washed and complaining bitterly about the whole business.

"Yer security light's on outside, yer know?" Jim settled himself back down on his stool

"I'd better go an' see if my missus has got anything they can wrap the babbie in" Dave muttered to himself, then realised what Jim had said. "Security light? What security light?" he asked "We haven't got a security light. I don't even know what a security light is when it's at home!" He hurried upstairs, calling his wife as he went. "Carol? Carol, love?"

"Bright as day out there" Jim muttered to himself.

Dave came back down the stairs, clutching a pile of what looked like old bandages.

"What yer got there, then?" Jim asked.

"Swaddling clothes" Dave said as he tried to sort the pile out into some sort of order.

"Swadlincote?"

"No, swaddling clothes, it was all the missus had got left"

"Seems a bit mean, dunnit?" Jim suggested

"Well, they should've brought their own, shouldn't they. Woman in that state, I don't know!" Dave said with exasperation, and swept out through the curtain with the pile of fabric in his arms.

"Nice little chap" he said when he came back in again, "adorable. Got his mother's eyes I reckon."

"Does 'e take after his dad though?" Jim asked, touching on a subject dear to his own heart.

"Difficult to say," Dave admitted, then lowered his voice, "not so's you'd notice, if I was being honest"

"Gerrus another then, Dave, might as well wet the babbie's head. Yer'd better get them two summat an' all, afore they kill each other or drive me mad on the way" Jim said generously, nodding in the direction of the shepherds before noticing they weren't there. "Where the 'eck did they go then?"

Dave parted the curtain, "Round the back to see the nipper, I think" he said, "d'yer wanter to see 'im?"

"Nah" Jim replied with feeling, "if yer've seen one, yer've seen 'em all. It's not as if he's owt special, is it?" He sipped his drink and considered, "Born in a stable eh?" he chuckled, "Well, I s'pose we've all got our cross to bear."

My Christmas Presence

It started as a clear, crisp day with that piercing winter sunshine that somehow switches the stark landscape from drab black and white to glorious Technicolor. I always think that Christmas should either be recently snow-covered or crisp, dry and full of sunshine. The worst possible types of Christmas are those with fog, ancient slush or that persistent drizzle that drapes the world like a cold sweat. This was one of those beautiful days that make you glad to be alive.

It was the late 1960's and we were at my Nana Whiteland's for Christmas Day Dinner. Nana and Granddad lived in a small terraced house, about halfway along Uxbridge Street, where they had spent their entire married life. The annual ritual of the gathering of the family for Christmas Dinner was a highlight of Christmas for me as a child. I loved my Nana's cooking. She was one of those all-purpose women that the early part of the last century seemed to breed. She was never still, always working and could do just about anything. From basic midwifery to the laying out of the dead and everything in between, my Nana was the person to call and many did.

I've mentioned before how much I particularly enjoyed the build up to Christmas at Nana's house. Before I started school, my afternoons were shared between my Nana Whiteland in Uxbridge Street and my other Nanny, my mum's mother, in Branston Road whilst my mum worked at Smith's Refrigeration as a secretary.

As Christmas approached, the pace of work at Nana Whiteland's increased. The whole thing usually started with the mixing of the cake. This was done in the living room, the small kitchen being entirely inadequate for such a serious undertaking. The whole dining table was cleared for the operation as packets and packets of ingredients were gathered together and a huge mixing bowl took centre stage. The smell that arose, as more and more fruit and liquor was added to the mixture, was wonderful.

I can still see the scene now, my grandmother labouring away over the mixing bowl with her wooden spoon, the fire crackling in the grate as darkness cloaked the yard outside, and her thin trebly voice giving a rendition of a popular song from the music halls of years ago. She had one of those singing voices that were common then but which you hardly hear now – after the style of Gracie Fields I think would be the best description.

I was, of course, allowed to help with the mixing, once the process had reached a point where it would be both physically possible for me and where I could do no major damage. A great delight would be sampling the uncooked mixture once the bowl had been emptied into the baking trays. Then the house was filled with the richest, Christmassy smell possible as the cake cooked slowly but surely in the trusty oven.

Cake making was not just restricted to Christmas. Nana would often provide cakes for weddings, christenings and other celebrations for family and friends and anyone else who had heard of her prowess. Icing, however, was not her forte and so the completed cakes were often packed up in tins and carried to a lady who lived in a small terrace of houses that used to exist at the back of the Blue Posts on High Street.

I used to enjoy accompanying her on these expeditions as the house of the Icing expert had a permanent smell of baking and I could stand outside and listen to the cacophony of sound that emanated from the brewery marshalling yard. This long-gone relic of the brewery steam train era used to exist, roughly where the Burton Place shopping centre is now, if memory serves me correctly.

However, I digress. On this particular Christmas Day the house was being prepared for the influx of family assembled for my Nana's Christmas feast. The table had been pulled from its usual place on the far wall, into the centre of the small room and had been extended. Chairs from all over the house had been pressed into service.

As a child, I was usually relegated to sitting on the arm of one of the nearby armchairs. These were the good, old-fashioned armchairs of yesteryear, the sort that could probably withstand a nuclear attack. The arms were of highly polished wood and sloped downward from the hand-rest to the back of the chair. I tended to start my meal at the highest point but then find that I was sliding remorselessly down the arm as the meal progressed. Thus, although I was high enough to negotiate my meal at the start, by the end I would virtually have my nose pressed against the table top.

Now, at the ripe old age of 14, I was detailed by my mum to accompany my dad on the present-giving round and then to the pub. The idea behind this was that I would be a sort of remote control nagging system. My purpose was to ensure that dad delivered the presents to various friends and family and then returned from the pub in time for the Christmas Dinner. This was a three-line whip. As mum was only too well aware, father had a somewhat relaxed attitude to time during licensing hours (except at the end of them).

After a short tour of various homes, delivering presents and cards and exchanging pleasantries, we moved on to the serious business of the day and headed toward the Union Inn in Union Street. Here, the landlord allowed me, on high days and holidays, to lurk in a back room whilst dad had a pint or two with his friends.

Normally this would involve a glass of lemonade and a packet of crisps, but this was Christmas. "Give the lad a drink", one of my dad's friends insisted and I opted for a half of cider. Over the next hour or so, as various customers passed by en route to the facilities outside, further drinks were pressed on me in the spirit of Christmas although, in all honesty, a great deal of pressing was not required.

My nagging potential was dipping in direct relation to my consumption of alcohol. I'm not sure if my dad realised quite how much I had consumed but we eventually set off for Uxbridge Street again, me filled with a deep and abiding love of the human race, beaming benignly at the children as they sped past on impossibly shiny bicycles or gleaming roller skates.

It was at this point that I made a fatal error. You may take the view that drinking cider on an empty stomach at the age of 14 was hardly a good move in the first place, but it got worse. An indulgent uncle had given me a small cigar. I was already consuming the occasional No. 6 tipped behind the bike sheds during the week, so I felt that I was sufficiently mature to handle this development. Dad knew that I smoked occasionally and took the view that, if allowed to continue, I would eventually get sick of it. He was wrong. Dad and I lit cigars and continued our walk home, filled with good spirits (in my case, cider) and the love of our fellow men.

By the time we reached Nana's, we were late and the rest of the family had gathered. Disapproving looks and pursed lips greeted our arrival but dad and I were impervious, shrouded in the bonhomie of alcohol. All together, I suppose there were about ten of us for dinner. The table was laid and groaning with all of the plates, cutlery and condiments. Wine glasses were in evidence.

Christmas was the only time that anyone ever drank wine in our family. My youngest uncle was the designated wine expert, on the tenuous grounds that he occasionally made home-made wine from such exotic basics as tea leaves and banana skins. The choice was almost always 'Tiger Milk', which I think was a Hungarian Liebfraumilch. This would usually be the only alcohol I would have contact with at Christmas, apart from the occasional liqueur chocolate.

For some unknown reason, on this particular Christmas Day, I had been positioned at the head of the table. I can still see the scene now. Relatives were ranked on both sides of me. In the distance, I could see my mum, although she was unaccountably blurred (perhaps she had been drinking). I was also aware that I was getting seriously warm.

In those days, we did not serve ourselves from tureens as we might do today, there simply would not have been enough space on the table. Instead, every possible option would be piled on the plate and you were expected to munch your way through as much as your constitution allowed, which had better be most of it. Various negotiations took place by shouting through to the kitchen, on the lines of "not too much cauliflower for me, please", "can I have a leg, please" or "don't give me any stuffing, you know how it serves me".

I was deemed to be a growing boy with a healthy appetite and, therefore, what arrived in front of me looked like a scale model of Mount Snowdon. Mashed potato dominated the centre of the plate and then, carefully positioned around this towering edifice was a chicken leg, brussel sprouts (I think there is some sort of law that states that you must have these at Christmas), cauliflower, sausage, roast potatoes, stuffing and so on and so on. At any other time it would have been a sight that would have filled me with joy. Not on this occasion, however.

I had already drunk my wine (another bad idea) and now my entire system seemed to go into revolt. I was covered in a cold sweat; the room buzzed and swirled around me. I had no choice. I rushed away from the table and dived for the first place available. Unfortunately, this was that 'holy of holies', the front room.

The front room at my Nana's house was for use on only two possible occasions, in the unlikely event of royalty coming to call, or on Christmas Day. The room was beautifully furnished and kept spotless but we were always clear that it was only to be looked at, not used. On Christmas Day (and only on Christmas Day) the fire would be lit, the lights would be on and we would be encouraged to make ourselves comfortable in a place that had never been designed for comfort.

Nana Whiteland in the sacrosanct Front Room at Christmas -
my mum and sister can be seen lurking behind her

It was in these hallowed surroundings that my intake of cider and cigars made an unexpected return appearance. To say that I was ill would be an understatement. Dad was despatched to take care of cleaning up operations and I collapsed into a little heap of misery and acute embarrassment. For me, Christmas Dinner was definitely over.

It was some time before I plucked up the courage to return to the family gathering. I thought that my presence would be very much frowned upon and I would be 'persona non grata' but I was actually received quite sympathetically. Father, on the other hand, was very much in the dog house for the rest of the day. I think that I can safely say that my contribution to that Christmas would come under the 'unwanted gift' heading.

That I was forgiven, and the rest of the day went smoothly, is a testament to the impossibly high spirit of human kindness that we all try to adopt each Christmas, and which usually fails miserably when the first toy becomes embedded in our bare foot at 5 in the morning.

I have this theory that the reason I cannot stick to a diet in my middle age is because my body believes that it has been robbed of a Christmas Dinner and is trying to compensate for this fact. It may not be much of a theory but it comforts me when I look down at the scales. Now, if you'll just warm that mince pie for me with perhaps a dash of cream, I'll be on my way.

Luncheon for One

It could be that, by the time you read this, Christmas will be over and done with and we'll be in that curious 'no man's land' between the jollity of Christmas and the full-on festivity of the New Year. People who were earnestly saying that they hoped you would "have a good Christmas", right up to Christmas Eve, will today just as earnestly be asking "Did you have a good Christmas? and you, like me, may well be wondering if you blinked and missed something vital in that brief two-day period that we spent months building up to.

You see (and I know this is going to characterise me as a cross between Ebenezer Scrooge and The Grinch), I really think that Christmas is a triumph of hope over experience. Christmas Lunch (or dinner, or supper I suppose, whichever you prefer) suffers from incredibly high expectations. For weeks in advance of 'the occasion' we are bombarded with images of smiling, happy family groups gathered around an impossibly large table. On this has been placed a golden, perfectly roasted, turkey which is about to be carved, in a highly professional manner, by the beaming Head of the Family. I don't know about you, but I have never been to a Christmas Lunch that looked anything like this.

Christmas Lunch is also a relentlessly social occasion. You are expected to be there and no excuses will be accepted. I have only once tried to avoid a Christmas Lunch, and I must admit to being surprised at how difficult it is to actually do this.

This dates back to when the present Mrs. Whiteland and I first met. When Christmas arrived, we had only been going out for a few weeks and didn't want to start a 'hare running' by announcing that we were going to spend Christmas Day together. Moreover, Hilary had family commitments to attend and we were not a public 'item' at this point.

We therefore decided that Hilary, and her daughter, Caroline, would go to the family Christmas Lunch in Birmingham but would return mid-afternoon, whereupon I would join them for Christmas Tea (this part of the plan not being for public consumption). My schedule was to have a simple lunch on my own, in my flat, watching the Christmas Television.

Announcing this caused consternation all round, on the lines of "you can't have Christmas Dinner on your own, come and have it with us, we've more than enough..." etc. I had to battle really hard to achieve my aim.

The strange thing is that, even though I knew I had only a few hours to wait before I would be enjoying my Christmas Day with the people I loved, sitting alone in my flat with my Turkey TV Dinner, I felt an immense sense of sadness, melancholy and isolation. I guess, in that short space of time, I had a glimpse of what it must be like for those without any choice in the matter and for who this is as good as Christmas is going to get.

For those who do find themselves alone this Christmas, can I wish you a much improved New Year and, just remember, at least you get to choose what television programmes to watch!

This is the 'AlterNativity' instalment which started it all...

A Stable Upbringing

The little enclave was rank with the heavy odour of animals and old straw. Dimly they could see a donkey and a couple of oxen but there was the sense of others in the darkness, pressing closer. In the centre of the picture the tired mother, agitated father and sleeping infant were lit by a glow that could not easily be attributed to the single candle, guttering in the draught.

They approached closer and one of their number (as always happens) found himself thrust forward, the other two peering over his shoulder and breathing heavily with the excitement of it all. There was a stirring in the manger, the infant screwed its face and contorted its body in preparation for a good cry, then thought better of it and resumed a peaceful sleep. The activity dislodged a swaddling band, the three edged closer.

They looked carefully. They looked at each other in wonderment. They shook their heads. Eventually, one spoke.

"It's a girl!" The lead spectator cried.

"Leave it out," the father said a little too quickly, "it's just cold, that's all."

"It is nippy." Another member of the party agreed.

"You are joking, I take it?" The lead spectator snapped. "I'm a wise man. Everyone agreed?" He glowered at the assembly until a muffled assent was obtained. "And I'm telling you, that's a girl." He drew himself up to his full height, the crown grated against one of the roof beams and a shower of dust and dead spiders fell gently around his face, utterly destroying the effect he was trying to achieve by glaring at the sweating father.

"Look, it's brass monkeys out there, innit?" The father hastily rearranged the swaddling bands. "You know how it is. And he's only little to start with."

"Just what are you trying to pull, eh?" The lead wise man was face to face now with the father. "We've travelled miles for this. On flaming camels! Have you any idea what that's like?"

"Been a few miles on the donkey," the father mumbled, "mind you, it's the missus's really. I've put me name down for a mule but I'm not holding me breath."

"Well, let me tell you, my good man, imagine having your innards removed with a corkscrew, by a drunk, in the middle of a storm at sea, and you're getting there. Not to mention what it does for your important little places" he sighed heavily, "'Except at least I've got some important little places to worry about. Which brings me back to the point at issue. It's a girl!"

The father shot a sideways glance at the mother. She

turned away quickly. He placed his arm as best he could around the towering shoulders of the lead king and manoeuvred him to one side.

"Look, keep your voice down can't you, you're upsetting the wife."

"It is a girl, isn't it?"

"Yeah, it's a girl; just don't go shouting the odds like that, eh?"

"Well, what the...what are you going to do about it?"

"Look, I'm doing my best, right? The wife's in a terrible state, she blames herself. I've been trying to get hold of an angel all night but can you get one when you want one? Oh dear me, no. All out with the heavenly host singing fit to burst aren't they? Plus, I've tried to get through to upstairs." He raised his eyes toward the dirt encrusted ceiling, "they're playing hell up there." He added confidentially.

"I'm not surprised!" The lead king affirmed, "This isn't what we were expecting."

"No, squire, you don't get my drift, I mean they're playing Hell up there. Some kind of celebratory cup match. Can't get a bit of sense out of them." He sighed. "Cos, this is what comes of leaving it to angels, if you ask me. Do you know who they went and told about all this first, eh? Eh? Bloody shepherds, that's all."

"Shepherds? I thought we were the first to know."

"No, not by a long chalk mate. We've only just got the place fit to walk in again. You know what shepherds are like, straight off the fields and in here without a 'by your leave', sheep sh*t all over the place, you've never seen nothing like it. Been all the same if we'd had a proper hotel room, which we could have had I might mention." He glared at the mother again.

"Oh, I understood…." The king began.

"Oh, I know what you understood. 'No room at the inn' and all that cobblers. You don't think I'd traipse all the way over here, with me missus expecting any minute, and not have a room booked do you? Got it all sorted hadn't I. Nice room with views of the star, en suite garderobe, gaps under the doors for air conditioning, just the ticket. Only, when we fetches up here and the gaffer comes out to take our luggage, the wife only pipes up 'Oh, we'd be as comfortable in the stable.' And here we are. Fine way to bring a kid into the world, I must say. She's got some very funny ideas since she was filled with the Holy Spirit – and don't get me started on that, I haven't begun to figure that one out."

"So our long and arduous journey has been wasted." The king looked despondent, his two companions were busy making 'goo goo goo' noises at the infant.

"Oh no, squire." The father spotted the glittering caskets each was carrying, "I'd stick around for a day or two. They're bound to sort it, ain't they? Mind you…" he considered for a moment, "you're a man of the world ain't you, an educated sort if you get my drift?"

"I am a wise man, yes. I've got a certificate somewhere." He rummaged through his robes.

"Course you are, that's what I'm saying, innit? Only, I could use a bit of advice. Come and have a look here, will you?"

The father led the way into the gloom of the rear of the stable.

"Runs in the wife's family apparently. You'd think they'd check up on these things but, oh no, it's all sing hallelujah, bash the tambourine and hang the consequences. Now then," he took a deep breath, reached into another manger and pulled back a crude blanket. "What do you reckon we should do about this?"

"Oh my God!" The king stared at the father, open-mouthed. "Twins?"

"Twins." The father confirmed.

Which made me think about the animals in the story and what they thought about it all? I think we have to assume that the 'difficulties' described in the last instalment have now been sorted out!

Get Away! In A Manger

The animals steamed and slumbered in the dark stable, occasionally shifting their weight from weary foot to equally weary foot, to get a little relief. The ox, in particular, was desperately trying to catch up on some sleep before the long day tomorrow. The ass, by his side, was wide awake.

"Waiter, waiter..." The ass began, hopefully.

The ox continued to slumber, or certainly appeared to do so. The ass stepped smartly sideways and banged into him, raising quite a cloud of dust and rousing the ox.

"What the h..." He quickly remembered the sleeping infant and started again, "just what do you think you're doing?"

"I said 'Waiter, waiter...'" The ass explained.

"Look, I'm not interested in your asinine jokes"

The ass looked at him reproachfully, as only an ass can.

"I speak as I find" the ox said, huffily "I wouldn't mind, but it wasn't funny the other fourteen times you told it!"

"Oh, go on. It's Christmas after all" The ass pleaded.

"That's another thing. Every time you come up with one of these dumb jokes, you come out with this stupid phrase *It's Christmas*. No-one knows what you're talking about!" The ox snorted loudly and stamped a hoof irritably.

"Just repeating what the humans have been saying all night, that's all" The ass sulked.

"So, what is this 'Christmas' then?"

"Seems to involve giving presents from the look of it. See, there's some gold, although I can't think what use that is. You can't eat it; I've tried and got yelled at." The ass said, gloomily. "There's also a couple of other things that make me sneeze if I get anywhere near them. Plus eating and drinking quite a bit, if those shepherds are anything to go by. Talking of eating...'Waiter, waiter'" The ass looked at the ox, expectantly.

"Oh, go on then." The ox sighed and adopted a resigned tone 'Yes sir, what seems to be the problem?"

"There's a baby in my soup" The ass's brays filled the stable

"It's not soup, It's hay" The ox pointed out

"Well, it's the same thing innit?" The ass snapped, "Wouldn't be soup in a manger now, would it? What use would that be, eh? I've adapted it for my species. You've just got no sense of humour, you."

"But it's just not funny!" The ox pointed out, "It's just a statement of the flaming obvious. Where did you get it from?"

"Out of a cracker" The ass muttered

"I reckon you've missed something, somewhere. Look, you've woken him up with your braying now." The ox observed.

"He's alright. He's not crying, is he? Ooza booful babyden, eh?" The ass leaned over his manger and addressed his remarks to the infant, who seemed to understand and gurgled appreciatively. "I just wish he'd hotch over and let me have a mouthful of hay. My stomach thinks my throat's been cut. I tried to snaffle a few strands a while ago and his mam had a fit."

"I'm not surprised, damn great nashers like yours chomping away by her son and heir" The ox snorted," enough to give anyone the vapours"

Just at that point, there was a terrific sound like a whole flotilla of ships lost in the fog. The ass skittered and the baby jumped a foot from his manger, but didn't make a sound.

"What the dickens was that?" The ass asked.

"Just the cattle lowing at the back" The ox replied, "Shut up, you morons, there's a baby here you know!" He yelled over his shoulder.

"Thought you would be joining in" The ass said, archly, "right up your street a spot of lowing, I would have thought"

"What do you mean by that?" The ox asked, menacingly.

"Well, they're all your lot aren't they?" The ass suggested, "Bovine" he added, with some distaste.

"Don't you dare lump me in with that lot" The ox bellowed to everyone's surprise, "They're cattle...kine...nothing to do with me. I'm a beast of burden" he ended proudly.

"So? That's me too. I can carry stuff. You just pull stuff along. Anyone can do that" The ass sniffed.

"Ah, but I'm specifically mentioned in the carols" The ox said, proudly.

"So am I" retorted the ass.

"But you get second billing. I'm the star!" The ox held his head a little higher and fluttered his eyelashes. "The ox and the ass, that's what it always says. I'm in Isiah too, and he knew what he was talking about"

"Bullocks!" the ass said, with feeling, "you're nothing but a potential jar of Bovril trailing a good bowl of soup. Just remember, I brought them here!"

"Oh yes, and don't we know it! Shepherds and all sorts traipsing in at all hours, Heavenly Hosts singing till the cows (begging your pardon, ladies) come home, not forgetting infants in your dinner. Nice one!" The ox pawed the ground agitatedly.

The ass considered a withering response but took a

deep breath, causing quite a few swaddling clothes to come unwrapped, and calmed down a little. "Speaking of dinner..." he nudged the ox again, "Waiter, waiter..."

"I'm not playing. Go and bother somebody else" The ox sniffed.

"There isn't anybody else. Have you ever heard of anyone else being mentioned, eh?" The ass pointed out with exasperation, "It's just you, me and your mates, the cattle, lowing"

"There's a lamb. The shepherds brought him. He must be wandering around here somewhere"

"You can't do jokes with a lamb. They just stand there looking cute and going 'baaa' winsomely" The ass grumbled.

"Well, I'm going to get some kip, so just shut up and leave me alone"

There was a long silence in which the ox attempted to settle down to a nap. His breathing had just taken on that regular rhythm that presages a good snore, when he was nudged heavily again.

"Wha...Now what?" He thundered

"I could do with a jimmy" The ass stated

"A what?"

"A jimmy. You know, a jimmy riddle...a widdle!"

"Well, go on then. I'm not stopping you" The ox said, reasonably.

"I don't like to. Not with the baby watching and everything. Doesn't seem right" The ass stated, primly.

"Well, it's up to you, but it hasn't stopped him, has it? Just look at the state of your hay" The ox nodded toward the manger.

"Oh no. He hasn't, has he?" The ass wailed.

"Looks like it" The ox chuckled, "do you good to lose a few pounds anyway"

The ass stared at the infant for a while, thoughtfully.

"What do you think he'll be when he grows up?"

"Who? The nipper?" The ox considered the question for a while, "Didn't his dad say he was a carpenter or something? Suppose he'll follow his dad. Do him good to have a trade behind him."

"Perhaps he'll make wooden DONKEYS for the kiddies to play with?" The ass suggested.

"Humph!" The ox replied, disdainfully. "With all these toffs bringing presents and the celestial choir and everything, maybe he's going to be something more than a carpenter?"

"What, like a cabinet-maker, something like that?" The ass suggested.

"Dunno. Could be." The ox tried to shrug his massive shoulders, unsuccessfully.

"Well, whatever, I'll take him wherever he wants to go" The ass declared, loyally.

"You want to be careful making promises like that, you never know where you might end up" The ox warned.

"If he does turn out to be a carpenter, perhaps, he could make you a yoke" The ass sniggered, "Speaking of jokes..."

"We weren't" The ox pointed out.

"Well, anyway, 'Waiter, waiter...'"

"Is there any chance of me getting a kip if I don't do this?" The ox asked, irritably.

"Nope"

"Oh for goodness sake, "Yes sir, what seems to be the problem?"

For some time now, I've been writing short stories involving two hapless undertakers, Josiah and Archibald. I couldn't fail to involve them at Christmas, could I?

Brightest and Best of the Sons of the Mourning?

In the yard at the rear of Oakshott and Underwood, 'Understanding and Sympathy at your time of need' (or, as Archibald Thurble once memorably amended it 'We Shift Stiffs') the proprietor of the Funeral Directors', Josiah Oakshott, was lovingly and carefully polishing one of his fleet of gleaming funeral cars. This was, by no means, one of his responsibilities. He just rather enjoyed taking a brief break from his usual concerns and indulging in this mindless but ultimately satisfying activity which gave him a great deal of pleasure. Pleasure that instantly disappeared at the sound of,

"Uh, Mr. Oakshott?"

The unmistakeable noise of an approaching Archibald Thurble clearly indicated that Josiah's peace was about to be shattered by one of his usual, and persistent, concerns. Josiah sighed deeply and turned to face his tormentor.

"Yes, Archibald, what can I do for you?"

"Egbert says you've taken down my Christmas window display!"

Egbert, in Josiah's opinion, really ought to mind his own business.

"I regret that is, indeed, the case Archibald and I am sorry that I did not have the time to discuss the matter with you before my action. I must say, I was surprised to find that you had taken it upon yourself to update our window display at all."

"Ah, well, I think I've found my forty, Mr. Oakshott!"

"Your forte? Have you indeed, Archibald, and what might that be, pray?"

"Oh no, it's nothing to do with religion" Archibald shook his head vigorously and tugged at the sleeve of his cheap dark suit, a sure sign of excitement or agitation in Josiah's experience. "I'm into Marketing."

"Marketing? Is that so? I was unaware you had studied the topic, Archibald."

"Oh yes, I've read articles. Well, I've read an article…and the title of another. My mum says that I've got a real flair for it" Archibald said, proudly.

"Yes, I'm sure she did. Tell me, Archibald, would this new-found yen for the arcane practices of Marketing have anything at all to do with Mrs. Bartlett suddenly springing up and yelling 'Bingo!' during yesterday's service?"

"Ah, it's funny you should mention that, Mr. O., 'cause I was reading as how every business should have its USB"

"USB? My understanding, limited though that is, was

that USB stood for Universal Serial Bus and applies to something technological that I do not pretend to understand. However, we do have our own fulsome supply of P.C.s, laptops and the like, so I would imagine we already have our USB, if not several?"

"Perhaps I've got that wrong!" Archibald conceded, "It's summat about having something that no-one else has got"

"Might I venture, Archibald, that you refer to a USP or unique selling proposition?"

"Do I? Oh, right. Well, one of them, anyroad"

"How does this relate to Mrs. Bartlett?"

"Now that's what I was coming to. You know how we see some of the same faces, week in, week out, at every funeral?"

"It is true that we do appear to have a coterie of regular attendees, for whatever reason"

"Well, I thought they ought to be encouraged, 'cause it fills up the pews when there's not many there"

"A laudable concern on your part, Archibald, although I am not entirely convinced that it falls within our remit"

"Well, that article what I read, it says you should 'encourage repeat trade by promoting loyalty to your brand via targeted marketing strategies'"

"Did it, indeed? And how does this theoretical concept manifest itself in actuality?"

"You what?" Archibald tugged his sleeve repeatedly.

"How did you apply this idea?"

"Oh, well, I thought about how newspapers get you to keep buying them..."

"Hmm, a useful analogy, Archibald, go on"

"So, I gave bingo cards to all of our regulars. When the vicar announces the number of each hymn..."

"It all becomes clear to me now, Archibald. As much as I admire your undoubted initiative and, I can assure you, I have no desire to crush your entrepreneurial spirit, nevertheless, I think this particular promotion is somewhat ill-advised and must be withdrawn forthwith"

"Ohh!" Archibald responded in the time-honoured tradition of a scolded toddler.

"It simply is not in keeping, Archibald. Not to mention the fact that it gave the Reverend Chapman one of his turns"

"What about my window dressing then?"

"Ah, yes" Josiah sighed, "I'm glad you mentioned that"

"All the other shops have a Christmas display" Archibald pointed out.

"Indeed they do, Archibald. However, we are not as other shops. We do not tout for trade, nor is Christmas different, in our profession, from any other time of the year, except that our clients may well need more support and understanding at such a poignant time"

"No fairy lights then?" Archibald asked, glumly.

"No, Archibald, although, oddly enough, the fairy lights were the least of my concerns"

"It's the crib scene, innit?"

"Well, not to put too fine a point on it, yes it is. Not that I have anything against nativity scenes, per se" Archibald looked puzzled. "In and of themselves" Further puzzlement, "In general!"

"Oh, right, so I can put it back then?"

"I fear not, Archibald. To be honest, the problem with the scene emanates from the nature of the crib itself. Because, it was not a crib as such, was it Archibald?"

"Well, no, not as such" Archibald admitted, reluctantly, "I made it myself, it took ever such a long time"

"And a fine piece of workmanship it was too, but that rather misses the point, because it was a ..." Josiah waited patiently for Archibald to complete the sentence.

"A miniature coffin" Archibald muttered, indistinctly.

"A miniature coffin! That is correct, Archibald. Tell me, did you have any concept at all of just how macabre a scene would be presented to the passing public by the sight of the Infant Jesus, lying in a miniature coffin?"

"I put the animals around and everything!"

"I appreciate that, Archibald, but that simply evoked the impression that they were, for whatever reason, attending a doll's funeral. We have had complaints, Archibald. Quite a number, in fact, even in the short time that your regrettable tableau graced our window"

"Pity they haven't got nothing better to do" Archibald grumbled.

"In some ways, Archibald, I am inclined to agree with you and yet, in others, I have to say that my faith in the basic good taste of the great British Public has been, to a certain extent, restored. That so many people should take offence at your depiction gives me hope for the future"

Josiah stood back and admired, for a moment, his polished handiwork. Then, tidying his cloths and polish into a wooden carry-case, he set off back to his office and the task of responding to the slew of complaints littering his desk.

"Alright, I'll tell you what, forget about the nativity" Archibald was at his shoulder as he progressed across the yard.

"Would that I could, Archibald. Regrettably, there is considerable correspondence on the subject that I have yet to address"

"No, what I mean is, how about summat else?"

"No, Archibald"

"I was thinking about a fairy on top of one of them urns perhaps?"

"No, Archibald"

"Alright, alright, how about some reindeer pulling a little hearse?"

"No, Archibald"

"Santa then? Santa on a...on a..." Archibald's mind raced, furiously, "on a cross!"

Josiah stopped and stared at him for a while.

"Have you any idea how many people that concept would offend, Archibald?"

"Not really, no"

"Nor have I, Archibald, and I have no wish to find out. Santa on a cross, indeed! Next you'll want the three wise men turning up with wreaths!"

"Ooh!" Archibald said, excitedly.

"No, Archibald"

THE END

Thanks very much for taking the time to read this book. I do hope that you have enjoyed the stories and that you now feel most decidedly ITCS, whatever that may be!

If you could spare a moment or two to leave a review, that would be great. It doesn't have to be a critical essay, just a few words to say what you thought of it.

If you would like to be amongst the first to know when any new books are being released, please send your name and email address to:

philwhiteland@philwhiteland.plus.com

Please also use this address for any questions or requests for information.

I promise that your details will never be shared with any third party, without your permission, nor will your data be used for any purposes other than for advising about any new writing by me, or in response to your queries. You can always unsubscribe at any time and details of how to do this will be contained in every email sent.

Looking forward to hearing from you.

Philip Whiteland, October 2018.

About the Author

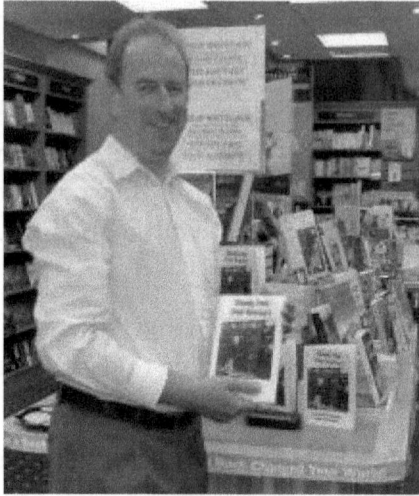

Philip at a book signing

Philip is a retired university lecturer based in the East Midlands. For much of his career he worked as a Human Resources Manager but he doesn't tell many people about this because their eyes tend to glaze over as he speaks. Mind you, that happens anyway, whatever he is talking about.

He lives with his wife and cat on the edge of the Derbyshire Peak District or, as he says, more accurately just lives on the edge. Philip has written a monthly article for the Bygones section of the Derby Telegraph and is constantly trying out new pieces in his blog, The Slightly Odd World of Phil Whiteland.

If you have nothing better to do, you can follow Philip on Twitter @philwhiteland or visit his Facebook page or contact him by email:

philwhiteland@philwhiteland.plus.com

Also by this Author

The Nostalgedy Collection

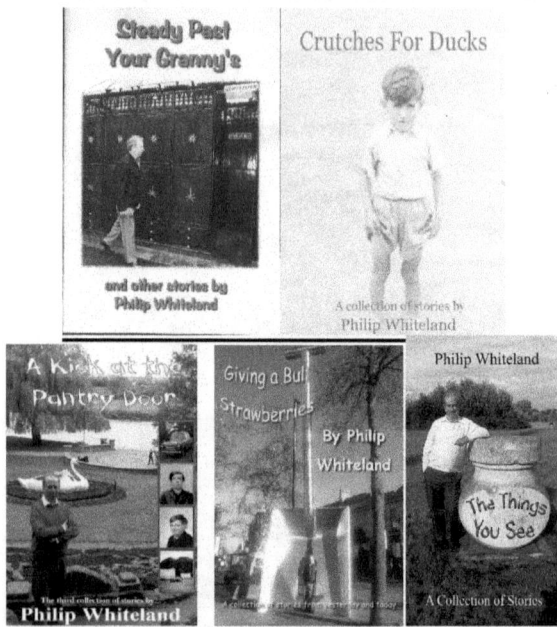

Five collections of stories, blending nostalgia about growing-up in the 1950s. 1960s and 1970s, with comedy...now read on

Find the whole collection at your local Amazon site by typing in this simple link:
http://mybook.to/nostalgedycollection

Steady Past Your Granny's

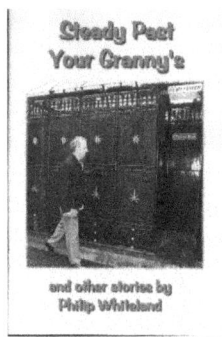

Take a trip back to a different place and time. Where crowds of hunched and oddly dressed youths would probably be train-spotters, where you could have a reign of terror on a Sunday afternoon just by riding your cast-iron scooter across the blue brick pavement, and where the height of excitement on the street was getting two Beech Nut chewing gum packets on the fourth turn of the handle.

Philip Whiteland entertains with some keenly observed and very funny meanders through the past and present. Come and join him on the trip, but, whatever you do, remember to keep "Steady Past Your Granny's"

Available as a Kindle edition
Find the book at your local Amazon site by typing in this simple link: **http://getbook.at/Grannys**

Crutches for Ducks

Enter the slightly odd world of Phil Whiteland and slip back a few decades to a time when a John Bull Printing Outfit was the height of toy technology, when the telephone never stretched more than two feet from the front door, when every boy's knee was covered by a three inch square of brown sticking plaster and when a trolley-bus into town was a great adventure.

This bumper collection of 'nostalgedy' stories (what happens when you mix nostalgia and comedy) coupled with some contemporary observations, guarantees a smile on every page and a chuckle in every chapter. Settle down for a step back in time and a giant leap forward in enjoyment, and if anyone asks you what you're doing, just tell them "Leos for meddlers..." (Complete with pictures - you have been warned!)

Available as a Kindle edition
Find the book at your local Amazon site by typing in this
simple link: **http://getbook.at/crutchesforducks**

A Kick at the Pantry Door

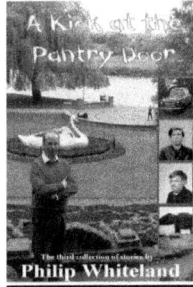

Philip Whiteland tickles your fancy (it's not a crime yet) once again with this compilation of stories, often with a food-based theme, from today and yesterday. Pull up a chair and tuck in! But first, a word from our Maitre d'Hotel:

"Welcome to the 'A Kick at the Pantry Door' restaurant. We have your favourite table ready and waiting and a selection of tasty and unusual dishes for your delectation and delight (but do bear in mind that the kitchen closes shortly as the Chef needs to go to his second job, rodding out blocked sewers). We have a few choice 'nostalgedy' stories for Starters, some meatier ones for your Mains, a selection of 'curmudgeonly rants' or keen observations (you take your choice) for Dessert, and something unspeakable to go with your Coffee and Mints.

What are the ingredients? Well there's: Our dog's unfortunate addiction to railwaymen - avoiding the great outdoors - how not to take a picture - unfinished business in woodworking - entries as an indicator of intoxication - mowing under pressure - Easter as a moveable feast - a regrettable incident at the Crucifixion. You won't find any E numbers, dodgy additives or nuts in our meals, unless of course you count the Chef."

"Taking the interesting theme of the reader being a visitor to a restaurant, Philip sets out his book in a number of chapters under the headings of starters, main courses, desserts and coffee and mints. All the stories relate to his experiences growing up in Burton in the 1950s and 1960s...A flavour for the amusing content of the book is given in the first chapter, in which Philip recalls his childhood interest in eating dog biscuits." Derby Telegraph

☐

Available as a Kindle edition
Find the book at your local Amazon site by typing in this simple link: **http://getbook.at/AKickatthePantryDoor**

Giving a Bull Strawberries

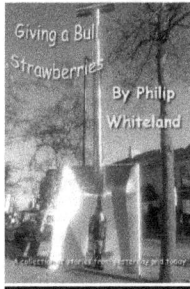

The fourth book in the ever popular 'nostalgedy' series of books. However, you don't need to start at Book 1 and work through to Book 4, or even start at Chapter 1 etc., you can dip in and out at will, and it will all make sense.

Yet another collection of tales from yesterday and today, designed to bring a smile to your lips (although I can't think of anywhere else you would want a smile) and a warm glow of recollection...wherever you fancy having a warm glow, I suppose.

They say that strategy is something that is only obvious in hindsight (I don't know who this 'they' is, but they seem to say a lot of things) but it is certainly true of this compilation. I was casting about for an overall theme for the stories when I realised that, one way or the other, the majority are about transport. Of course, I've now decided that this was my intention all along!

Armed with an overarching theme, the structure for the book just had to be after the style of the old Highway Code, which I remember poring over, first for my Cycling Proficiency Test and later for my Driving Test (and have never looked at it again since). Do you remember the old

Highway Code? It used to have separate sections for the different road users, such as The Road User On Foot, The Road User On Two Wheels and so on. Well, if it was good enough for the Highway Code, it's definitely good enough for me. Hence this compilation is split into sections covering The Author on the Road, The Author on Rails, The Author at Sea and, finally, The Author at Large, which is a catch-all description of everything that I couldn't shoe-horn into the other three sections.

In these sections you will experience, amongst other things; the dubious delights of flat, warm beer at 08.30 in the morning as you set off by train for Blackpool, the horrifying sight of three less than agile people crossing the M5 on foot, the three-year slog of endeavouring to learn to drive and the trials of trying to find a working cash machine in Malaga in the wee small hours. All of these stories, and many more besides, are yours for the reading.

"*Philip Whiteland brings his own special brand of nostalgic humour to a new book which has just been published. The fourth book in his amusing "nostalgedy" series, it carries the eye-catching title Giving a Bull Strawberries.It comprises a collection of tales from yesteryear and today and promises to bring a smile to people's lips along with a warm glow of recollection.*" Jane Goddard, Derby Telegraph

Available as a Kindle edition
Find the book at your local Amazon site by typing in this simple link: **http://getbook.at/BullStrawberries**

The Things You See...

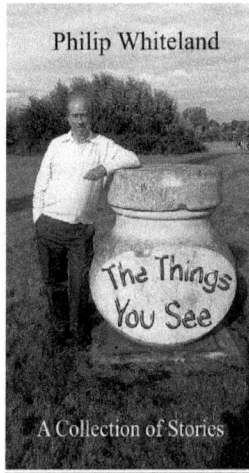

Philip Whiteland

The Things You See

A Collection of Stories

Philip's back with a fifth collection of stories, both 'nostalgedy'(a mixture of nostalgia and comedy) and other observational pieces in which he takes a wry look at times past and present.

Every book has to have a theme and the structure for this one came whilst he was idly munching a chocolate bar. You know that one which used to promise to help you work, rest and play? Well, this book consists of Work, Play and the Rest.

In '**Work**' Philip joins the ranks of the employed at the beginning of the 1970s, firstly as an inept packer of plastics before moving to 'a nice dry job with no heavy lifting' in a dark, satanic paper mill. We learn about his struggles with punctuality, the difficulties of working in the darkness of the 3-Day-Week and why he had a real reason to be grateful for Ted Heath.

'**Play**' brings tales of a boozy holiday in Franco's Majorca in the 1970s, a fleeting role in a 'Look at Life' documentary, Cilla Black, Soap Operas, an insight into the Cultural Quarter of Stoke-on-Trent and some tales from a trip to Australia.

Finally, '**the Rest**' shovels up everything that wouldn't fit into the first two, including a tour around a pub in the 1960s, getting a brace fitted at the dentist's, difficulties with sanitary arrangements, why grass should be left alone, why shopping with your wife is an overrated pastime, a grumble about grammar and why it is absolutely fine to be a NIMBY. All wrapped up with the Title article, which is not for the faint-hearted.

Come and join Philip in his Slightly Odd World, you won't regret it!

Available in both Print and Kindle editions
Find the **Kindle** version at your local Amazon site by typing in this simple link:
http://mybook.to/ThingsYouSee

Find the **Print** version at your local Amazon site by typing in this simple link: **http://mybook.to/PrintThingsYouSee**

You can also order online via Waterstones:
https://www.waterstones.com/book/the-the-things-you-see/philip-whiteland/9780955431012
or order in store at any local bookshop.

In the event of any difficulty, please contact the author at:

philwhiteland@philwhiteland.plus.com

www.ingramcontent.com/pod-product-compliance
Lightning Source LLC
Chambersburg PA
CBHW061731020426
42331CB00006B/1195